GW00792539

CONTENTS

...As Superman	6
The Pest from The Fifth Dimension	7
Business as Usual	8
...And Oh So Delicious!	9
The Toyman's Christmas List	31
Ninety Days Later...	32
Men Of Steel	33
What Would You Do If You Were Superman?	56
Another Ninety Days Later...	57
The Scoop Of The Century	58
The Oldest One In The Book	59
Superman's Power Trip	81
A Week In The Life Of Lois Lane	82
All In A Day's Work	83
Yet Another Ninety Days Later	84
(Almost) The World's Finest Team	85
Mr Action	107
Supergirl's Secret Emergency Weapon	108
While You Were Sleeping	109

Published by Pedigree Books under licence from DC Comics.

© 2000 DC Comics. All Rights Reserved.
All characters appearing in this book, including their names & distinctive likeness & all related indicia, are trademarks of DC Comics.

SUPER DC HEROES

ANNUAL 2001

Pedigree®

Published by Pedigree Books Limited
The Old Rectory, Matford Lane, Exeter, EX2 4PS

£6.99

IN THE PLANET KRYPTON'S FINAL MOMENTS, AN INFANT WAS SENT OFF IN A ROCKETSHIP.
THE SHIP CRASH-LANDED ON EARTH, IN AN AMERICAN TOWN CALLED SMALLVILLE, AND WAS DISCOVERED BY JONATHAN AND MARTHA KENT.
THE KENTS WOULD TAKE THE INFANT IN AS THEIR OWN...
...AND AS CLARK KENT GREW OLDER, HE LEARNED THAT EARTH'S YELLOW SUN AND LIGHTER GRAVITY HAD GIVEN HIM AMAZING POWERS.
NOW LIVING IN THE CITY OF METROPOLIS, CLARK WORKS AS A NEWSPAPER REPORTER FOR THE DAILY PLANET.
HE ALSO FIGHTS FOR TRUTH AND JUSTICE ACROSS THE WORLD-- AND BEYOND--
JULY IV
...AS SUPERMAN
SUPERMAN CREATED BY JERRY SIEGEL & JOE SHUSTER
WRITER: MARK MILLAR
INKS: TERRY AUSTIN
LETTERS: PHIL FELIX
COLORS: MARIE SEVERIN
SEPS: ZYLONOL
EDITS: MIKE McAVENNIE
PAGE 1 PENCILLED BY TY TEMPLETON

SUPERMAN ADVENTURES 41. March, 2000. Published monthly by DC Comics, 1700 Broadway, New York, NY 10019. POSTMASTER: Send address changes to SUPERMAN ADVENTURES, DC Comics Subscriptions, P.O. Box 0528, Baldwin, NY 11510. Annual subscription rate $23.88. Canadian subscribers must add $12.00 for postage and GST. GST # is R125921072. All foreign countries must add $12.00 for postage. U.S. funds only.
Copyright © 2000 DC Comics. All Rights Reserved. All characters featured in this issue, the distinctive likenesses thereof, and all related indicia are trademarks of DC Comics. The stories, characters and incidents mentioned in this magazine are entirely fictional.
Printed on recyclable paper. Printed in Canada. DC Comics. A division of Warner Bros.–A Time Warner Entertainment Company

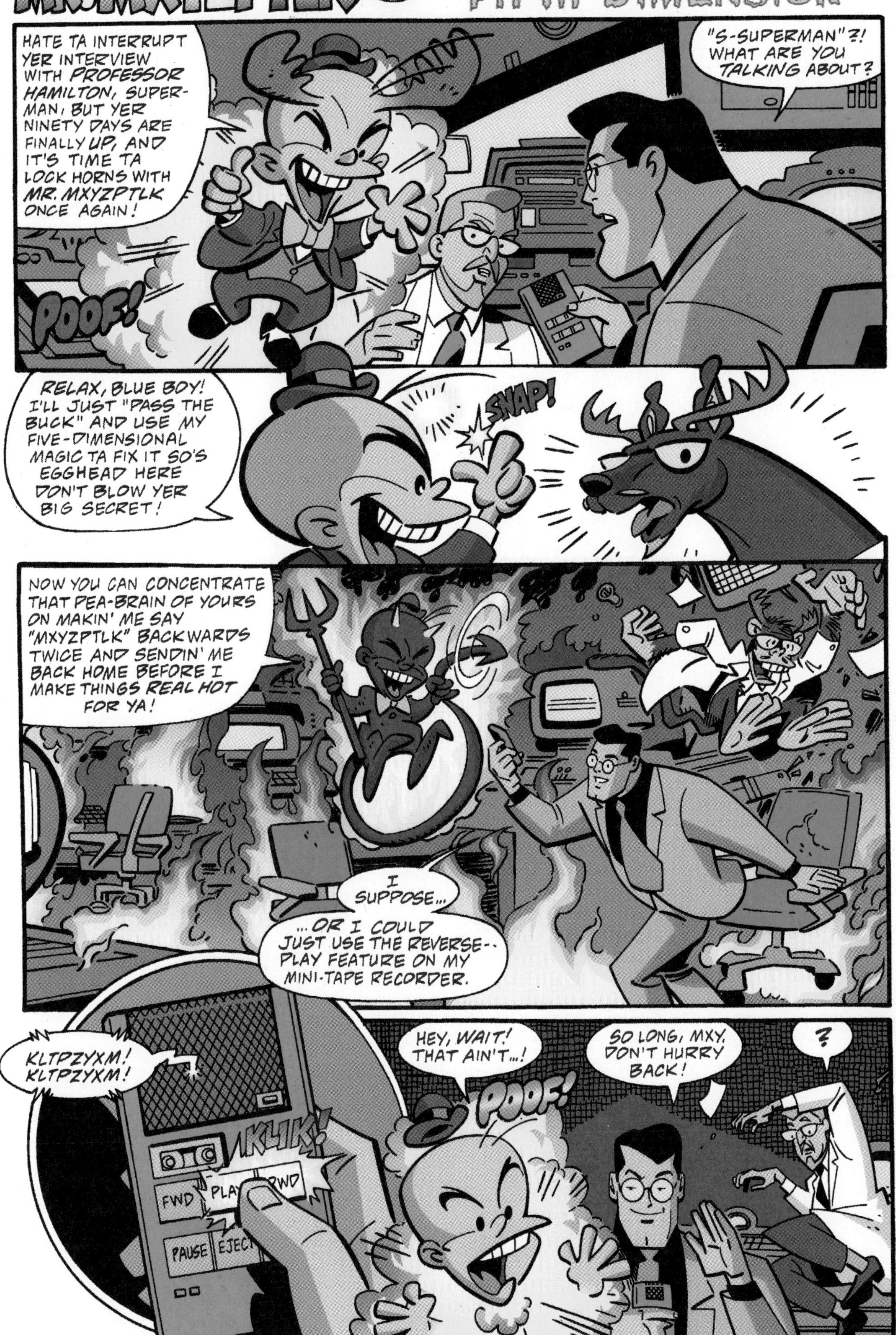

PENCILLER: JOE STATON

LEX LUTHOR IN "BUSINESS AS USUAL"

PENCILLER: MIN S. KU

WHAT'D I TELL YOU? NOT A SINGLE HITCH.
...And Oh So Delicious!
SCOTT PETERSON-writer
TIM LEVINS-penciller
TERRY BEATTY-inker
LEE LOUGHRIDGE-colorist
TIM HARKINS-letterer
JOSEPH ILLIDGE-associate editor
DARREN VINCENZO-all natural
BATMAN created by BOB KANE

BATMAN: GOTHAM ADVENTURES 20. January, 2000. Published monthly by DC Comics, 1700 Broadway, New York, NY 10019. POSTMASTER: Send address changes to BATMAN: GOTHAM ADVENTURES, DC Comics Subscriptions, P.O. Box 0528, Baldwin, NY 11510. Annual subscription rate $23.88. Canadian subscribers must add $12.00 for postage and GST. GST # is R125921072. All foreign countries must add $12.00 for postage. U.S. funds only.

Copyright © 2000 DC Comics. All Rights Reserved. All characters featured in this issue, the distinctive likenesses thereof, and all related indicia are trademarks of DC Comics. The stories, characters and incidents mentioned in this magazine are entirely fictional. Printed on recyclable paper.

Printed in Canada.
DC Comics. A division of Warner Bros.–A Time Warner Entertainment Company

DON'T EVER POINT A GUN AT ME.
YEAH, OKAY.

ARE THEY BOTH SECURED?
TIED UP PRETTY AS YOU PLEASE. WOULDN'T SAY A THING, THOUGH.
DOESN'T MATTER. WE'LL KNOW IN A MOMENT WHAT THEY WERE STEALING.

WINTER'S COMING-- I'M BETTING FURS.
OR MAYBE GOLD FOR THE HOLIDAYS.
NO, WAIT... IT'S...

IT'S...

Eden's Own
IT'S CEREAL?
Eden's Own

WOW, I KNEW EDEN'S OWN WAS POPULAR, BUT I HAD NO IDEA IT'D GOTTEN THIS BIG.
SO YOU'VE HEARD OF THIS CEREAL BEFORE?
ARE YOU KIDDING? EDEN'S OWN IS THE HOTTEST THING ON THE MARKET. THERE'RE A LOT OF PEOPLE WHO WON'T EAT ANYTHING ELSE.
I FIRST HEARD ABOUT IT FROM BATGIRL--IT'S ONLY SOLD THROUGH HEALTH FOOD STORES, SO COLLEGE KIDS WERE ABOUT THE FIRST TO PICK UP ON IT.
THESE DAYS, THOUGH...
WELL, JUST TAKE A LOOK.
THE STORE WON'T EVEN BE OPEN FOR FIVE HOURS AND PEOPLE ARE ALREADY LINING UP TO BUY THE STUFF.
BLOSSOM HEALTH FOODS
WE HAVE EDEN'S OWN!

PARDON THE INTRUSION, FRIEND, BUT ARE THESE THE OFFICES FOR EDEN'S OWN?
Eden's Own
THEY ARE, BUT I BELIEVE THEY ACCEPT DELIVERIES IN THE BACK.

Oh, THAT'S OKAY. I'M HERE TO GET A JOB.
A JOB?
YEAH, I KNOW, BUT THERE'S A FIRST FOR EVERYTHING. I JUST THINK THIS IS A WORTHY PLACE FOR MY FIRST JOB, YOU KNOW?

QUITE, BUT MY POINT IS, THERE ARE TWO DOZEN APPLICANTS WITH MBA'S IN FRONT OF YOU. WHY, I RECEIVED MINE AT HARVARD AND --
unh!
HEY!

YOU WANNA START SOMETHIN'?
NO WAY, DUDE. IT'S COOL.

I LIKE HOW YOU HANDLED YOURSELF BACK THERE.
HEY, VIOLENCE DOES *NOT* LEAD TO HARMONY.
A FEELING SHARED BY MOST OF US HERE.
SO YOU'RE LOOKING FOR EMPLOYMENT? DO YOU HAVE EXPERIENCE?
LIKE, YOU KNOW THOSE PEOPLE WHO CLIMB TREES AND STAY UP FOR, LIKE, MONTHS SO LOGGERS CAN'T CUT 'EM DOWN?
YOU DID THAT?
NO, BUT I WROTE THEIR PRESS RELEASES.
WELL, I THINK WE CAN FIND A PLACE HERE FOR A PERSON OF YOUR TALENT.
Oh, AND LET ME INTRODUCE YOU TO THE GENIUS BEHIND OUR LITTLE COMPANY...

POISON IVY? SHE'S BEHIND EDEN'S OWN?
I WAS A BIT SURPRISED AS WELL.
I GUESS IT MAKES SENSE.
WHY'S THAT?
WELL, YOU KNOW, THE WHOLE POINT OF THE CEREAL IS THAT IT'S ULTRA-NATURAL AND HEALTHY.
IT'S GOT NO SWEETENERS OR PRESERVATIVES OR ANYTHING.
THAT'S WHY I FIRST HEARD OF IT MONTHS AGO. A LOT OF MY FRIENDS ARE TOTALLY INTO THE MACROBIOTIC SCENE.
EDEN'S OWN IS SUPPOSED TO MAKE YOU FEEL FANTASTIC-- YOU KNOW, "FEELS GOOD BECAUSE IT IS GOOD." WHATEVER.
NOT YOUR PHILOSOPHY?

I WISH IT WERE, BUT... WHAT CAN I SAY? I WAS RAISED ON SUGAR-FROSTED COCOA BOMBS.
THAT SOUNDS WORSE THAN WHATEVER IVY'S UP TO.
HEY, WHO KNOWS? MAYBE SHE'S REALLY JUST TRYING TO GET RICH AND MAKE PEOPLE EAT HEALTHIER.
I'M SURE YOU'RE HALF RIGHT.

HEY, I JUST FINISHED READING THAT COVER COPY YOU WROTE FOR THE NEW BOXES. GOOD WORK, MY FRIEND.
THANKS, DUDE. KIND OF A TRIAL BY FIRE, RIGHT?

LISTEN, SPEAKING OF TRIALS, THIS STUFF *HAS* ALL BEEN TESTED, YEAH?

YOU'RE KIDDING, RIGHT?
Uh... WHY WOULD I BE?

MY FRIEND, WHEN YOU'RE CLIMBING MOUNT EVEREST AND YOU MELT SOME SNOW TO QUENCH YOUR THIRST, DO YOU TEST IT FIRST?

AND WHEN YOU'RE DEEP IN THE RAINFORESTS OF THE AMAZON AND YOU FIND A LUSCIOUS MANGO, DO YOU TEST IT FIRST?
NO.

NO.
OF COURSE NOT.
ALL THE INGREDIENTS IN EDEN'S OWN ARE FROM THE BOUNTIFUL EARTH AND ARE GOOD FOR YOU BY THEMSELVES, ARE THEY NOT?

SURE.
SO HOW COULD THEY BE ANYTHING BUT GOOD FOR YOU WHEN THEY'RE COMBINED?

I DON'T KNOW, DUDE, BUT YOU'VE SOLD ME.
THAT'S WHAT WE LIKE TO HEAR.

AM I TRULY HEARING YOU RIGHT, MASTER BRUCE?
I'M AFRAID SO, ALFRED.

I CAN'T FIND A THING WRONG WITH IVY'S CEREAL.

Eden's Own
IN FACT, IF IT DIDN'T COME FROM IVY, I'D EAT IT MYSELF.

Eden's Own
3
Live
Eden's Own
I SEE THAT HER RALLIES ARE NOW TELEVISED.
CLEARLY, MOST OF THE POPULATION DOES NOT SHARE YOUR CONCERN ABOUT THE CEREAL'S ORIGINS.

THE EARTH IS GOOD. IT IS THE ORIGINAL MOTHER.
Eden's Own
YES!
LOVE YOUR MOTHER!
Eden's Own

AND MOTHER KNOWS BEST, DOESN'T SHE? YOU CAN'T IMPROVE UPON HER WISDOM.
Eden's Own KUDOS
SHE KNOWS!
WE ♥ Eden's Own
SHE IS WISE!

WE CAN FEEL IT! WE LISTEN!
YOU ALL KNOW THIS DEEP INSIDE -- YOUR BODIES CAN FEEL THE TRUTH OF EDEN'S OWN COURSING THROUGH YOUR VEINS, TELLING YOU TO LISTEN TO THE EARTH.

THAT'S WHY WE'VE GOT PEOPLE WORKING DAY AND NIGHT TO PRODUCE MORE OF THE CEREAL YOU'LL DO ANYTHING FOR.

Whoa!

LISTEN, GUYS, TAKE ANYTHING YOU WANT. IT'S COOL.
IN FACT, PETTY CASH IS IN A CUPBOARD BY THE JAVA MACHINE AND--

WE'VE GOT WHAT WE CAME FOR.
HEY, THIS STUFF'S JUST LYING AROUND EVERYWHERE. DON'T SUPPOSE THEY'D MIND IF I HELPED MYSELF TO--

COULDN'T LEAVE WELL ENOUGH ALONE, COULD YOU?
YOU COULD HAVE HAD ALL THE MONEY, THE COMPUTERS, WHAT-EVER YOU WANTED, BUT THAT WASN'T ENOUGH, WAS IT?
NOW GIVE ME BACK MY EDEN'S OWN.

SOMETHING'S WRONG.

YOU'VE CHANGED.

IT'S JUST THE STRESS OF THE JOB.
NO, IT'S NOT.

YOU'VE HAD FAR MORE STRESSFUL JOBS BEFORE. THIS IS A VACATION COMPARED TO MOST.
WHAT DO YOU WANT?

YOUR BLOOD.

WHAT?

JUST RELAX.
IT'LL ALL BE OVER IN A MOMENT.

Eden's Own
...AND IF THE DISTRIBUTORS CAN'T HANDLE THE INCREASED--
WELL, WELL. I'M SORRY, KERI, I'M GOING TO HAVE TO CALL YOU BACK.

THIS BETTER BE IMPORTANT, BATMAN. I WAS JUST ABOUT TO CLOSE ON THE ASIAN MARKETS.
I THINK YOU'LL BE CLOSING ENTIRELY.

I COULDN'T FIGURE IT OUT AT FIRST. THERE WASN'T A THING WRONG WITH YOUR CEREAL. IT WAS PERFECTLY SAFE.

UNTIL IT WAS EATEN.

ITS EXISTENCE IN PEOPLE'S SYSTEMS SOMEHOW MADE THEM EXTREMELY SUSCEPTIBLE TO YOUR SUGGESTIONS, DIDN'T IT?
WHY NOT? EDEN'S OWN IS MADE UP ENTIRELY OF ORGANIC MATTER, MATTER THAT I CAN CONTROL.
ONCE IT'S DIGESTED AND REACHES THE PITUITARY, I SIMPLY HAVE IT RELEASE ENDORPHINS AT THE SOUND OF MY VOICE.
VERY WELL DONE, BATMAN. I DIDN'T EXPECT YOU TO FIGURE IT OUT FOR MONTHS YET.
YOU SEE, THAT'S WHEN EDEN'S OWN WOULD HAVE BEEN AVAILABLE WORLDWIDE.
WHICH IS WHEN I WOULD HAVE "SUGGESTED" THAT, FOR THE GOOD OF THE PLANET, THEY ALL "EXTERMINATE" THEMSELVES.
SOMETHING THEY WOULD HAVE GLADLY DONE.
THE POPULATION THUS DECIMATED, EDEN WOULD HAVE RETURNED.
WITH YOU OUT OF THE WAY, IT MAY YET.

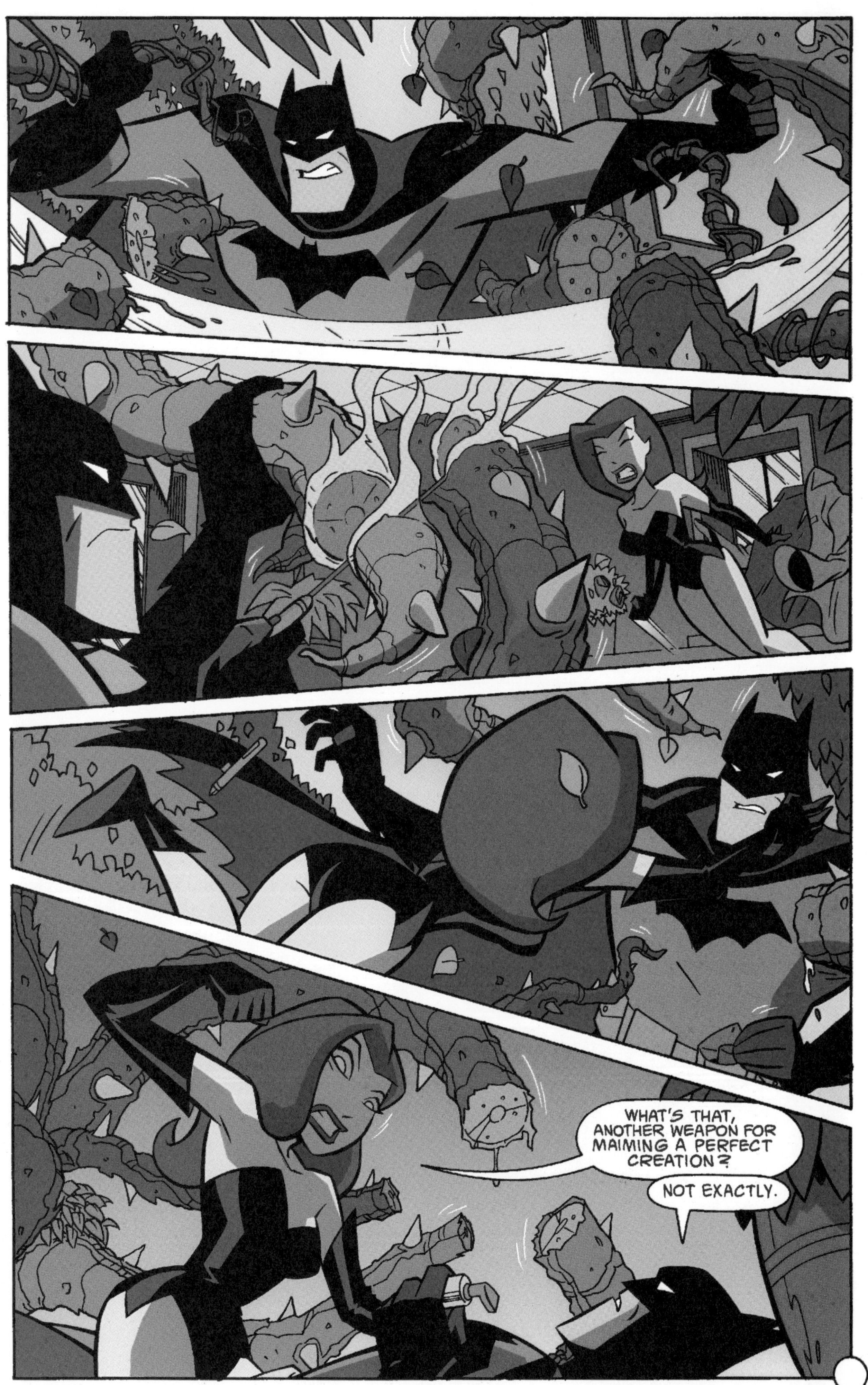
WHAT'S THAT, ANOTHER WEAPON FOR MAIMING A PERFECT CREATION?
NOT EXACTLY.

IT'S ALMOST NOTHING, REALLY.
JUST A LITTLE OXYGEN.
BUT... BUT... PLANTS DON'T... NEED OXY... OXYGEN...
PLANTS NEED CARBON DIOXIDE.
NO, PEOPLE DO.

...SO REMOVING ALL THE CARBON DIOXIDE FROM THE ROOM WORKED?
YES. THANKS FOR YOUR HELP.
Eden
Ow

NO PROBLEM. I WISH I COULD HAVE BEEN DONE MORE.
I'M... I'M SORRY I LOST CONTROL A LITTLE BIT.
IT WASN'T YOUR FAULT, NIGHTWING. IT WAS THE CEREAL.

I DON'T AGREE. I SHOULD HAVE KNOWN MY BODY BETTER. I SHOULD HAVE KNOWN WHEN I STARTED TO LOSE CONTROL.
ah... A FORMER FAN OF EDEN'S OWN. I CAN TELL.
BE HONEST NOW-- YOU'RE SORRY YOU FOUND OUT, AREN'T YOU?

I'M SORRY IT TURNED OUT NOT TO BE TRUE.
The End

"THE TOYMAN'S CHRISTMAS LIST"

"DEAR SANTA. I'VE BEEN A BAD BOY THIS YEAR AND OBVIOUSLY WON'T GET ANY TOYS, BUT THAT DOESN'T MEAN I WON'T BE SENDING GIFTS TO A FEW SELECTED FRIENDS...
"...LIKE SOME CRAZY PUTTY FOR THE JUDGE WHO SENTENCED ME TO LIFE ON STRYKER'S ISLAND...

"...A RADIO-CONTROLLED CAR FOR LOIS LANE...

"...AND A FEW TOY AEROPLANES FOR SUPERMAN WOULD MAKE THIS THE MOST PERFECT CHRISTMAS EVER!"

HEY, TOYMAN! DON'T FORGET TO ORDER A GIFT FOR THE GUYS WHO LOOK AFTER YA TWENTY-FOUR HOURS A DAY!
YEAH...HA-HA...PRISON GUARDS NEED TO KNOW THEY'RE APPRECIATED TOO, YA LITTLE FREAK.
OH, DON'T WORRY ABOUT THAT, GENTLEMEN...
...I'M SURE SANTA HAS SOMETHING EXTRA-SPECIAL IN HIS SACK FOR YOU BOYS.

PENCILLER: DARWYN COOKE

"NINETY DAYS LATER..."

MEN OF STEEL
Paul Dini - Writer
Rick Burchett - Penciller
Terry Austin - Inker
Marie Severin - Colorist
Lois Buhalis - Letterer
Mike McAvennie - Editor
SUPERMAN CREATED BY JERRY SIEGEL AND JOE SHUSTER
"In three years on the Planet's city desk, covering everything from gun running to garbage strikes...
"...this reporter had never seen anything like it."

SUPERMAN ADVENTURES 1. November, 1996. Published monthly by DC Comics, 1700 Broadway, New York, NY 10019. POSTMASTER: Send address changes to SUPERMAN ADVENTURES, DC Comics Subscriptions, P.O. Box 0528, Baldwin, NY 11510. Annual subscription rate $21.00. Canadian subscribers must add $12.00 for postage and GST. GST # is R125921072. All foreign countries must add $12.00 for postage. U.S. funds only. Copyright © 1996 DC Comics. All Rights Reserved. All characters featured in this issue, the distinctive likenesses thereof, and all related indicia are trademarks of DC Comics. The stories, characters and incidents mentioned in this magazine are entirely fictional. For advertising space, contact: East Coast, Tom Ballou, (212) 636-5520; Midwest, The Graffiti Group (312) 527-4040; West Coast, The Berman Company (818) 865-9708. Printed on recyclable paper.
Printed in Canada.
DC Comics. A division of Warner Bros.–A Time Warner Entertainment Company

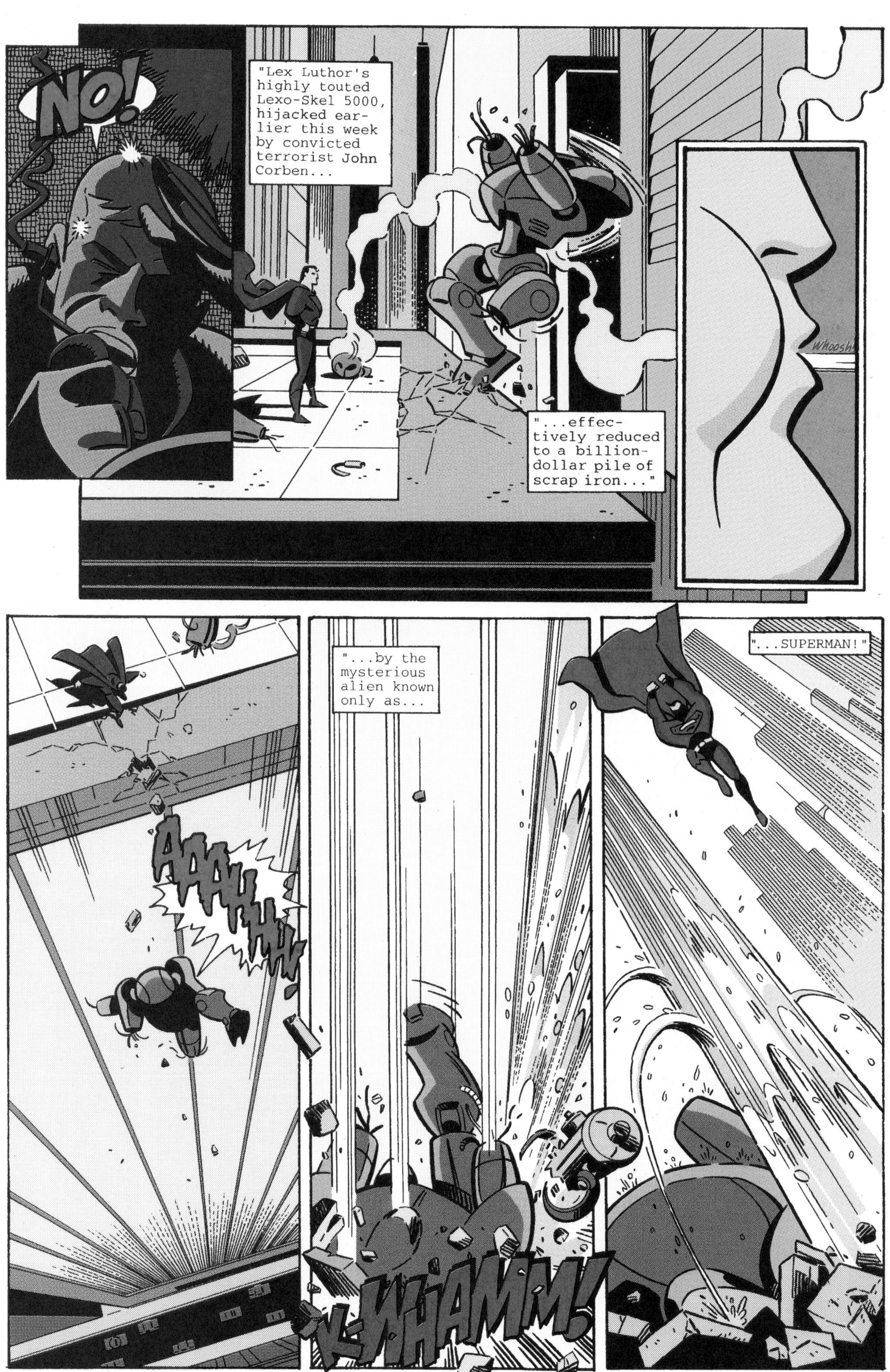
NO!
"Lex Luthor's highly touted Lexo-Skel 5000, hijacked earlier this week by convicted terrorist John Corben...
"...effectively reduced to a billion-dollar pile of scrap iron..."
Whoosh
"...by the mysterious alien known only as...
"...SUPERMAN!"
AAAHHHH!
K-WHAMM!

SHALL WE GO A FEW ROUNDS *WITHOUT* THE SUIT?
N-NO...!
TOO BAD!
"Under the circumstances, Corben opted to surrender without protest...
"...and was delivered into police custody."
YES, CHIEF, I THINK STOPPING THE PRESSES WOULD BE A *VERY* GOOD IDEA!
"AS FOR THE SO-CALLED 'MAN OF STEEL,' HE AND HIS PRESENT WHERE-ABOUTS CONTINUE TO REMAIN A MYSTERY."
NICE WORK, LOIS. BUT AREN'T YOU LAYING ON THE MYSTERY ANGLE A LITTLE *THICK?*
MAYBE IT'S JUST THE *CYNIC* IN ME, PERRY, BUT WHAT DO WE *REALLY* KNOW ABOUT SUPERMAN?

SURE, HE SEEMS TO HAVE EVERYONE'S BEST INTERESTS AT HEART, BUT AS A REPORTER, I NEVER TAKE ANYONE AT FACE VALUE...
...ESPECIALLY IF THEY CAN FLY!

CAN'T BLAME YOU THERE. WHAT ABOUT YOU, RON? ANGELA?

I THINK IF SUPERMAN HAD AN ULTERIOR MOTIVE, WE'D HAVE SEEN IT BY NOW, CHIEF. HE'S ONLY BEEN IN TOWN A FEW DAYS AND ALREADY HE'S SAVED DOZENS OF LIVES.
THE GUY'S DEFINITELY FOR REAL.
DAILY PLANET

YOU CAN SAY THAT AGAIN! SUPERMAN'S THE HOTTEST STORY TO HIT METROPOLIS IN YEARS!
I'M RUNNING EYEWITNESS ACCOUNTS IN MY COLUMN, PLUS EXCLUSIVE FOOTAGE OF THE BIG GUY IN ACTION ON TONIGHT'S "METROPOLIS EDITION."

AND I GOT SOME GREAT SHOTS OF HIM PUTTING OUT THAT FIRE LAST NIGHT IN SUICIDE SLUM!
I COULD LET YOU HAVE THEM IN EXCHANGE FOR, Oh, I dunno, A JOB ON THE PHOTO STAFF?
YOU NEVER QUIT, DO YOU, OLSEN?

I'LL GIVE YOU FIFTY BUCKS.
SOLD!
AND WHAT ABOUT YOU, KENT? I KNOW YOU'RE THE NEW GUY ON THE CITY DESK...

...BUT WHAT ARE YOUR THOUGHTS ON OUR STRANGE VISITOR FROM ANOTHER PLANET?

SORRY, PERRY. I'M AFRAID I HAVEN'T HAD ENOUGH CONTACT WITH SUPERMAN TO FORM AN OPINION.

WELL, LET'S STAY ON THIS, PEOPLE.

OUR READERS WANT INFORMATION ON SUPERMAN AND THEY WANT IT *NOW!*

Y'KNOW, THESE PHOTOS REALLY AREN'T BAD.

THANKS, CHIEF!

DON'T CALL ME CHIEF!

INFORMATION!

THAT WILL BE OUR MOST POTENT WEAPON IN THE BATTLE AGAINST THIS THREAT, THIS... "SUPERMAN."

HOW FORTUNATE MY PEOPLE WERE ABLE TO SALVAGE THE MEMORY UNIT FROM THE LEXO-SKEL'S COMPUTERIZED BRAIN.

NOW I CAN STUDY SUPERMAN IN ACTION AND PLAN MY ATTACK AROUND HIS LIMITATIONS.

I TRUST WHAT I CAN CONTROL. THIS CITY, FOR INSTANCE.
METROPOLIS WAS NOTHING UNTIL I REBUILT IT ACCORDING TO MY VISION. NOW MOST OF ITS PEOPLE WORK FOR LEXCORP OR ONE OF ITS MANY SUBSIDIARIES, AND THE CITY'S FEW VOICES OF DISSENT, SUCH AS S.T.A.R. LABS AND THE DAILY PLANET, ARE ALLOWED TO EXIST SIMPLY BECAUSE THEY AMUSE ME.
ALL IN ALL, IT'S A PERFECT PICTURE OF ORDER.
BUT SUPERMAN REPRESENTS A THREAT TO THAT ORDER. HE COULD CONFUSE PEOPLE, MAKE THEM UNCERTAIN OF WHO REALLY HAS THEIR BEST INTERESTS AT HEART--AN ALIEN WITH FREAKISH POWERS, OR ME, THE TRUE MASTER OF METROPOLIS.
THE PEOPLE MUST BE SHOWN IN NO UNCERTAIN TERMS HOW DANGEROUS THIS ALIEN CAN BE.

WELL, THORNTON?
WE'VE JUST COMPLETED THE SYNTHETIC SKIN ADHESION, Mr. LUTHOR.
YOUR "MAN OF STEEL" IS READY FOR INSPECTION.
...BUT TO SURPASS THEM!
ALL OF THEM? FLIGHT? SPEED? INVULNERABILITY?
AS YOU INSTRUCTED, WE'VE PROGRAMMED THE ANDROID TO NOT ONLY DUPLICATE SUPERMAN'S KNOWN POWERS...
YES, SIR. EVEN AN ADVANCED LASER SYSTEM TO SIMULATE SUPERMAN'S HEAT VISION.
EXCELLENT.

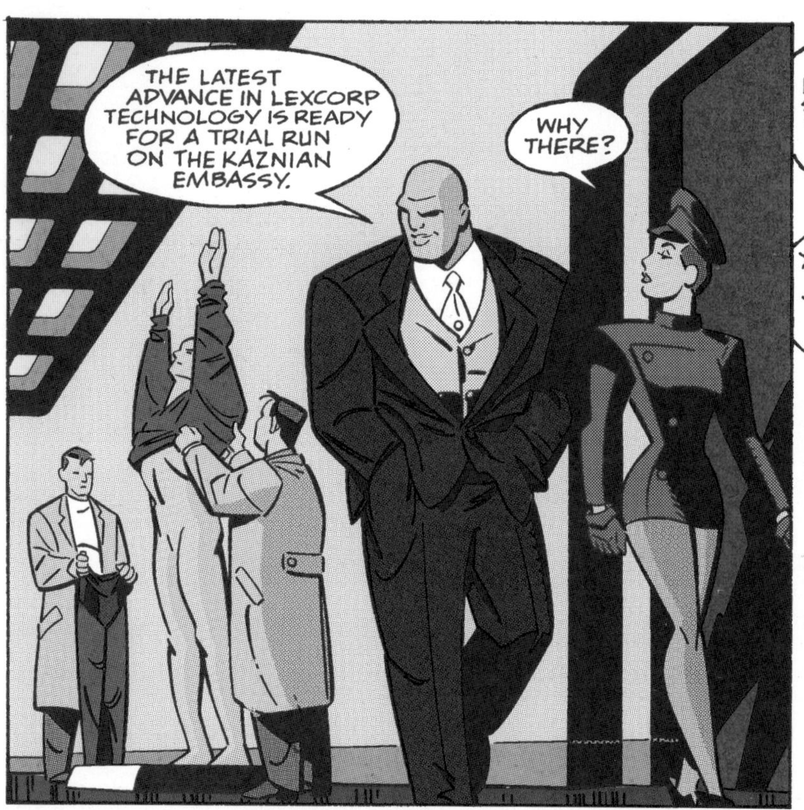

THE LATEST ADVANCE IN LEXCORP TECHNOLOGY IS READY FOR A TRIAL RUN ON THE KAZNIAN EMBASSY.
WHY THERE?

HAVE YOU FORGOTTEN THE REGENT OF KAZNIA STILL REFUSES TO PAY THE BILLION DOLLARS FOR MY *LEXO-SKEL 5000*?
EVEN THOUGH CORBEN FAILED TO DELIVER IT, I *INSIST* ON COMPENSATION.
SO YOU'RE SENDING YOUR OWN "SUPERMAN" TO SETTLE THE ACCOUNT.

"EXACTLY."

SUPERMAN SPEAKS!

Exclusive Interview by Lois Lane

FLYING MAN SAVES JET

SUPERMAN FO
TERRORIST

LOOKS LIKE YOU'VE MADE QUITE A NAME FOR YOURSELF, SON.

AND WHAT A NAME--"SUPERMAN"! I DON'T KNOW IF I'LL EVER BE ABLE TO SAY IT WITHOUT LAUGHING!
I LIKE IT. Oh, IT MIGHT BE A LITTLE GRAND, BUT I THINK IT GIVES FOLKS SOMETHING TO BELIEVE IN.

IF YOU SAY SO, MA. I JUST HOPE I CAN LIVE UP TO EVERYONE'S EXPECTATIONS.
NOW DON'T GO WORRYING HOW TO PLEASE EVERY-BODY.

YOUR MA'S RIGHT, CLARK. THAT'S A JOB NOT EVEN SUPERMAN CAN HANDLE.
JUST DO THE BEST YOU CAN, SON. I DON'T THINK ANYONE EXPECTS MORE OF YOU THAN THAT.
THANKS, PA. AND AS LONG AS YOU MENTIONED JOBS...

"...IT'S TIME I WAS GETTING BACK TO MINE."

DAILY PLANET
MA AND PA ARE RIGHT. EVEN WITH MY POWERS, I CAN'T BE EVERYWHERE AT ONCE.
BUT AS CLARK KENT, STAFF REPORTER FOR THE DAILY PLANET, I CAN KEEP MY FINGER ON THE PULSE OF WORLD EVENTS...
STORE ROOM
...AND THEN GO AS SUPERMAN TO WHERE I'M NEEDED MOST.
THERE YOU ARE, KENT!
WHERE HAVE YOU BEEN-- ON ANOTHER PLANET?
I ZIPPED HOME FOR LUNCH. WHAT'S UP?
PLENTY! WE JUST GOT A CALL...
...SUPERMAN'S ATTACKING THE KAZNIAN EMBASSY!
WHAT?!?

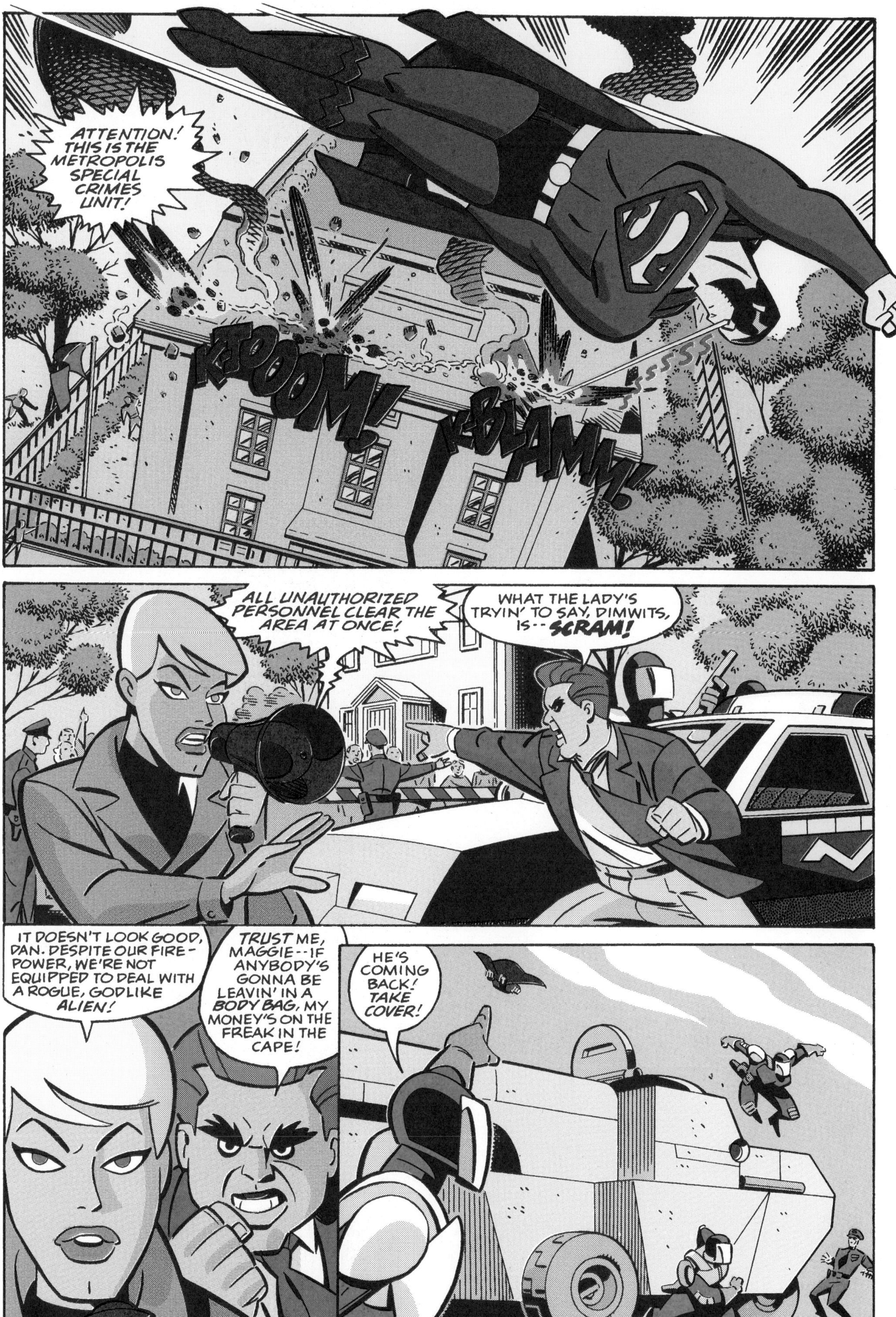

ALL UNAUTHORIZED PERSONNEL CLEAR THE AREA AT ONCE!

WHAT THE LADY'S TRYIN' TO SAY, DIMWITS, IS-- **SCRAM!**

IT DOESN'T LOOK GOOD, DAN. DESPITE OUR FIRE-POWER, WE'RE NOT EQUIPPED TO DEAL WITH A ROGUE, GODLIKE ***ALIEN!***

TRUST ME, MAGGIE--IF ANYBODY'S GONNA BE LEAVIN' IN A ***BODY BAG***, MY MONEY'S ON THE FREAK IN THE CAPE!

HE'S COMING BACK! TAKE COVER!

KRAASHH!!
BRATT-TAT-TAT
HIT HIM HIGH, BOYS!
BRING HIM DOWN ANY WAY YOU CAN!
K-BLAAM!
THIS IS AN ACT OF **BLATANT TERRORISM** AGAINST THE PEACE-LOVING KAZNIAN PEOPLE!

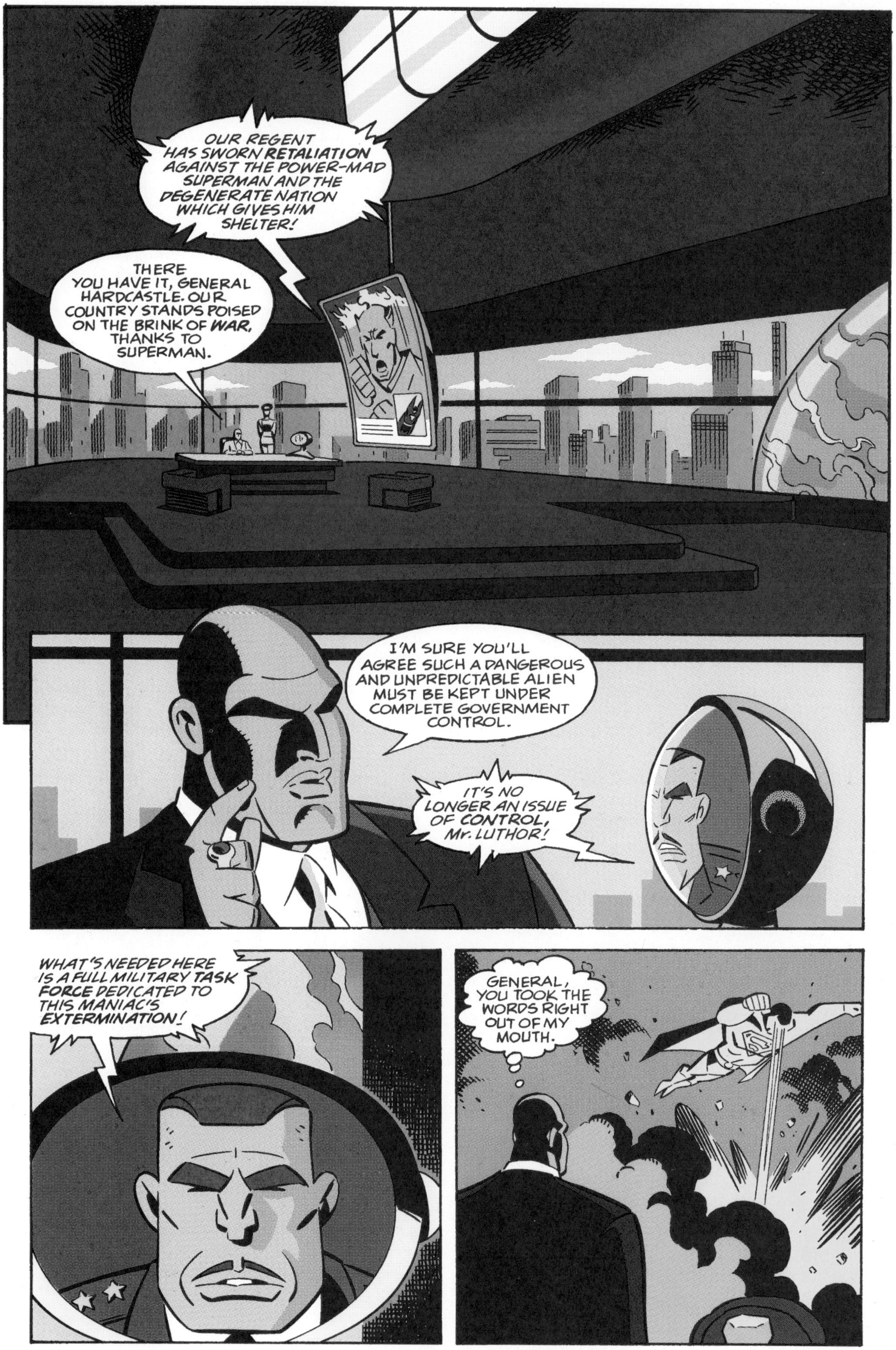

OUR REGENT HAS SWORN **RETALIATION** AGAINST THE POWER-MAD SUPERMAN AND THE **DEGENERATE NATION** WHICH GIVES HIM SHELTER!

THERE YOU HAVE IT, GENERAL HARDCASTLE. OUR COUNTRY STANDS POISED ON THE BRINK OF ***WAR***, THANKS TO SUPERMAN.

I'M SURE YOU'LL AGREE SUCH A DANGEROUS AND UNPREDICTABLE ALIEN MUST BE KEPT UNDER COMPLETE GOVERNMENT CONTROL.

IT'S NO LONGER AN ISSUE OF **CONTROL**, Mr. LUTHOR!

COME *ON*, TURPIN! LET ME THROUGH!
I SAID *NO REPORTERS*, LANE! THAT GOES *DOUBLE* FOR *YOU*!

LOIS CAN HANDLE THE POLICE WITH HER USUAL TACT AND DIPLOMACY.
FORTUNATELY...
I'LL MAKE SURE YOU GET A SPECIAL MENTION IN MY ARTICLE, DAN! HOW DO YOU SPELL "*THICKHEAD*"?
DON'T PLAY TOUGH WITH *ME*, MISSY!
...I HAVE *ANOTHER* OPTION.
WHATEVER DID THIS WAS BIG, POWERFUL, AND UNLESS I MISS MY GUESS...
...STILL IN THE AREA!

SSSSSSS
UNNGH!

SCORE ONE FOR MY JOURNALISTIC INSTINCTS!

THUMP THUMP THUMP THUMP
SOME KIND OF ROBOT...!

IT SEEMS YOU'VE MET YOUR MATCH, SUPERMAN.
KLANG!
LUTHOR!

THANKS TO THE MEMORY UNIT I PLACED IN THE LEXO-SKEL, I WAS ABLE TO GET AN ACCURATE GAUGE OF YOUR STRENGTHS AND WEAKNESSES.
I PROGRAMMED MY MAN OF STEEL TO NOT ONLY DUPLICATE YOUR POWERS...
KRASSHH
...BUT DOUBLE THEM.
THAT'S IT, SUPERMAN. FIGHT BACK. EXHAUST YOURSELF.
YOU'RE UP AGAINST AN ENEMY YOU CAN'T DEFEAT.
HE'S EVERY BIT YOUR SUPERIOR IN SPEED...
...STRENGTH...

...AND INVULNER-ABILITY.
MY SUPERMAN ALSO INCLUDES A FEW OPTIONS NOT FOUND ON THE ORIGINAL "MODEL"...
...SUCH AS REINFORCED RESTRAINING CLAMPS...
...AND A HIGH-FREQUENCY SONIC CHARGE, DESIGNED TO BLISTER YOUR SUPER-HEARING...
...AND DESTROY WHAT-EVER REMAINS OF YOUR RESISTANCE.

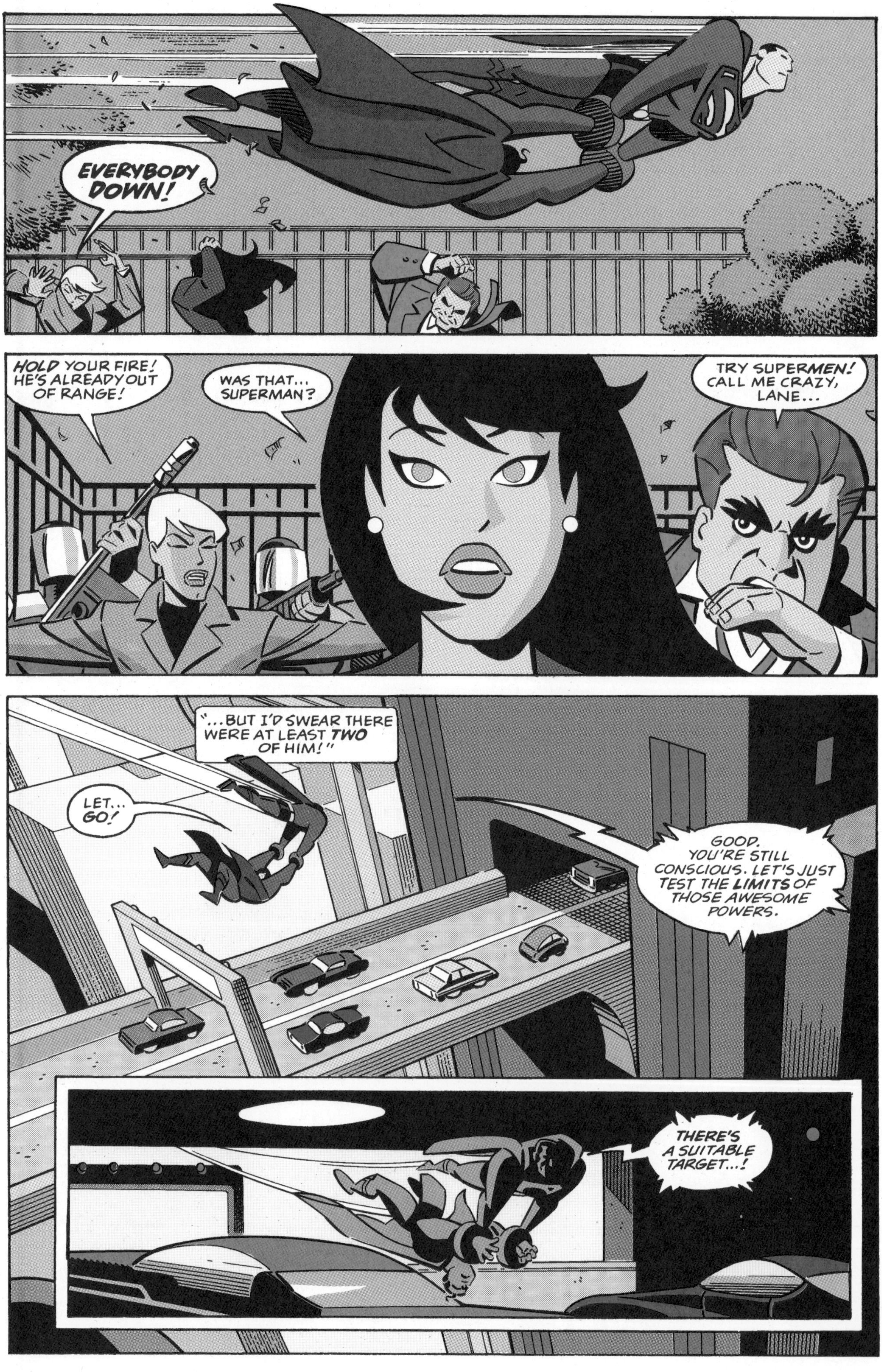

"...BUT I'D SWEAR THERE WERE AT LEAST TWO OF HIM!"

LET... GO!

GOOD. YOU'RE STILL CONSCIOUS. LET'S JUST TEST THE LIMITS OF THOSE AWESOME POWERS.

THERE'S A SUITABLE TARGET...!

PINK!
PANK!

STILL BREATHING, ALIEN? YOUR STAMINA IS NOTHING IF NOT IMPRESSIVE.
WHOOM!
HERE'S ANOTHER TRICK YOU'LL LIKE!
SSSZZT!
Oh, YES. YOUR HEAT VISION.

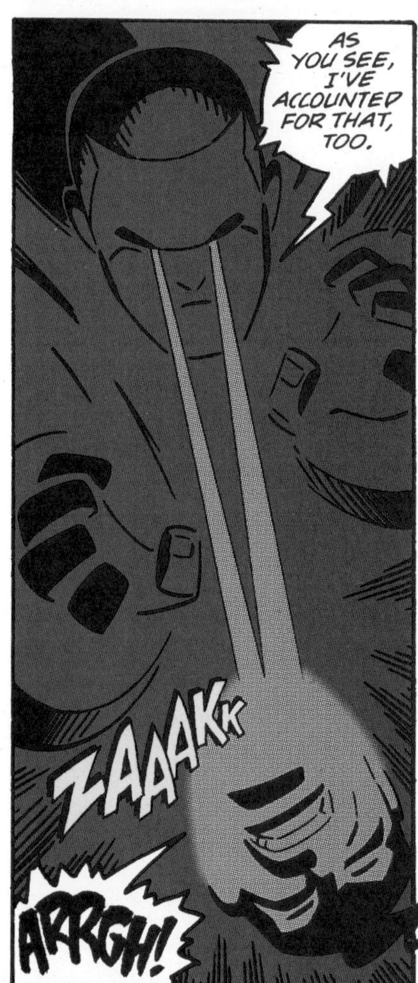
AS YOU SEE, I'VE ACCOUNTED FOR THAT, TOO.
ZAAAKK
ARRGH!

AND WHILE YOU MAY BE POWER-FUL, I'M REASONABLY SURE YOU CAN'T SURVIVE UNDER WATER.
THIS IS HOW IT ENDS THEN, SUPERMAN. YOU ARE DISPATCHED AS QUICKLY AS YOU ARRIVED.

A CURIOSITY, A FREAK, THAT CAUGHT THE PUBLIC'S EYE FOR A MOMENT, THEN VANISHED, LEAVING ONLY AN UNPLEASANT MEMORY.
FAREWELL.

I THINK NOW WOULD BE A GOOD TIME TO MAKE GENERAL HARDCASTLE AN OFFER ON MY LATEST LINE OF DEFENSE ANDROIDS.
YOU NEVER KNOW WHEN A HOSTILE ALIEN MIGHT TURN UP.

LUTHOR, HERE, GENERAL. THE SUPERMAN THREAT HAS BEEN NEUTRALIZED.
UH, LEX? LEX!

HE'S FREE!

NO!
IT'S NOT POSSIBLE!
LUTHOR? LUTHOR? ARE YOU THERE?

GET A SECURITY TEAM UP HERE NOW!

LASERS, GRENADES, GAS BOMBS--I WANT EVERYTHING!
LEX!

B-RAMM!
GET DOWN!

I COULD HAND THIS OVER TO THE POLICE, ALONG WITH A FORMAL COMPLAINT. NATURALLY, I'M SURE YOU'D GET THE CASE THROWN OUT.
STILL, THE ACCOMPANYING STORM OF BAD PRESS WOULD BE TOUGH FOR EVEN THE GREAT LEX LUTHOR TO LIVE DOWN.
YOU CAN'T THREATEN ME!
I'M NOT THREATENING. JUST SUGGESTING THAT THIS WHOLE UGLY BUSINESS WAS STAGED BY DISGRUNTLED EX-LEXCORP EMPLOYEES...
SNAPT!
...WHO SAW A CHANCE TO EMBARRASS US BOTH BY CREATING AN INTERNATIONAL INCIDENT.
SKRUNCH!
OF COURSE, YOUR PERSONAL APOLOGY, ALONG WITH A GENEROUS DONATION TOWARD REBUILDING THE KAZNIAN EMBASSY, WOULD HELP SMOOTH THINGS OVER.
YOU'VE GOT IT ALL WORKED OUT, HAVEN'T YOU?
IT'S THE BEST OPTION FOR BOTH OF US, LEX. BY CLEARING ME, I'LL REGAIN THE TRUST OF THE CITY I'M TRYING TO HELP.
OF COURSE, THAT'LL LEAVE YOU FREE TO TAKE ANOTHER SHOT AT ME...
...BUT I CAN DEAL WITH THAT.
SKRANKK!
SKRNNK!
SKRNNK!
YOU'RE VERY SURE OF YOURSELF, ALIEN. WHAT MAKES YOU THINK YOU'VE GOT THE UPPER HAND?

BECAUSE TODAY YOU REALLY BELIEVED YOU SAW ME AT THE LIMIT OF MY POWERS. SORRY, LUTHOR...
K-RASSH!

...I WAS ONLY AT THE LIMIT OF YOURS!
END

"WHAT WOULD YOU DO IF YOU WERE SUPERMAN?"
I'M ANGELA CHEN, AND TODAY WE'RE ASKING THE PEOPLE OF METROPOLIS: "WHAT WOULD YOU DO IF YOU WERE SUPERMAN?"
ME? SUPERMAN? SHEESH, I'D BE KING OF TH' WOILD! NO NUKES, NO ARMIES FIGHTIN' EACH OTHER, NONE'A IT. I'D SHOW EVERYBODY WHO'S BOSS, AND THEY'D LEARN TA GET ALONG PEACEFULLY. OR ELSE.
JOE OBLOGATZ
CAB DRIVER
ARE YOU KIDDIN'? I'D DO MY HOMEWORK AT SUPER-SPEED! MEBBE I WOULDN'T EVEN HAFTA GO TO SCHOOL! AND MOM COULD NEVER FORCE ME TO EAT MY VEGGIES!
JESSICA LUND
SUPERMAN FAN
SUPERMAN'S A SHOW-OFF. ASK ME WHAT I'D DO IF I WERE SOME-ONE LIKE LEX LUTHOR. THERE'S A MAN WITH REAL POWER WHO I WANT TO EMULATE.
JOHN CARLSTON
BROKER
ME, SUPERMAN? WELL, TO BE HONEST, I AM SUPERMAN.
SO ARE YOU, AND ALL THE PEOPLE WATCHING THIS. TEACHERS IN SCHOOL. POLICEMEN AND FIRE-MEN ON DUTY. PARENTS TAKING CARE OF THEIR KIDS. ALL THESE THINGS MAKE US SUPERMEN.
CLARK KENT
REPORTER
STILL...
...FLYING SOUNDS REAL APPEALING TO ME.
PENCILLER: NEIL D. VOKES

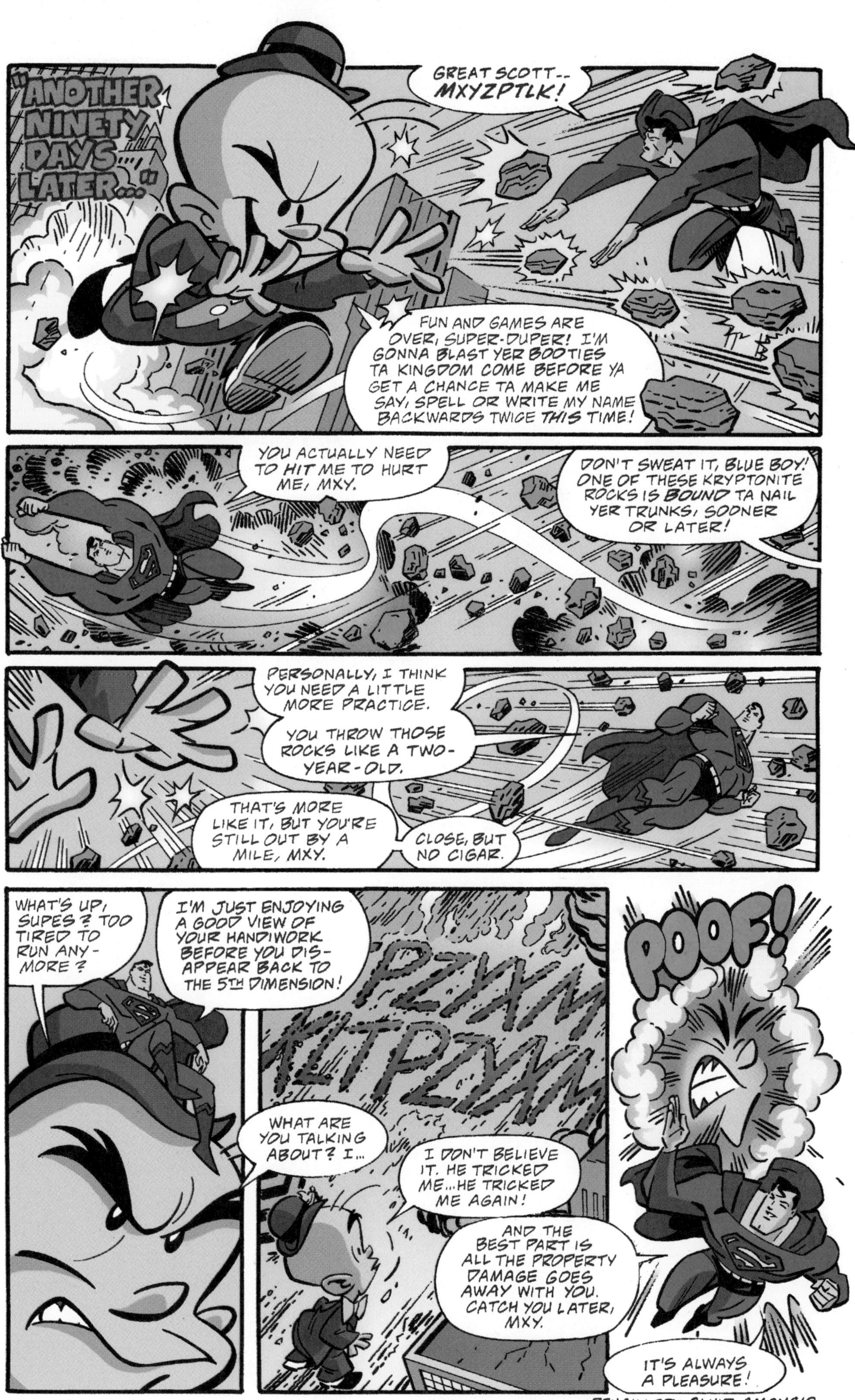

PENCILLER: ALUIR AMANCIO

"THE SCOOP OF THE CENTURY"

WORKING LATE:
MAN, SOMETIMES IT FEELS LIKE I'VE BEEN A CUB REPORTER FOREVER. I WISH I COULD FIND A GREAT STORY TO PUT ME ON THE MAP...

INVESTIGATING LEXCORP'S SHADY, INTERNATIONAL TERRORIST CONNECTIONS WOULD BE COOL, BUT THOSE CHEAPSKATES IN ACCOUNTING WON'T EVEN COVER MY BUS-FARE TO GOTHAM CITY.
DAILY PLANET

A PSYCHOLOGICAL PROFILE ON METALLO MIGHT HAVE BEEN AN AWARD-WINNER IF CLARK HADN'T DONE THAT PARASITE PIECE LAST YEAR.

MAYBE THERE'S A FRESH ANGLE ON SUPERMAN. PERRY'S ALWAYS SAYING HOW MUCH PEOPLE LOVE SUPERMAN STORIES...

WHERE DOES HE GO WHEN HE ISN'T SAVING PEOPLE? IS THERE A SIDE OF HIM NOBODY KNOWS? IS IT POSSIBLE HE'S EVEN GOT SOME KIND OF SECRET IDENTITY HE KEEPS QUIET ABOUT...?
DAILY PLANET

AH, FORGET IT, OLSEN...

PENCILLER: PHILIP BOND

heh heh... CHARLES BAXTER, AS I LIVE AND BREATHE.
hmm ?
TY TEMPLETON WRITER
RICK BURCHETT PENCILLER
TERRY BEATTY INKER
LEE LOUGHRIDGE COLORIST
TIM HARKINS LETTERER
JOSEPH ILLIDGE ASSOC. EDITOR
DARREN VINCENZO EDITOR
BATMAN CREATED BY BOB KANE
THE OLDEST ONE IN THE BOOK!

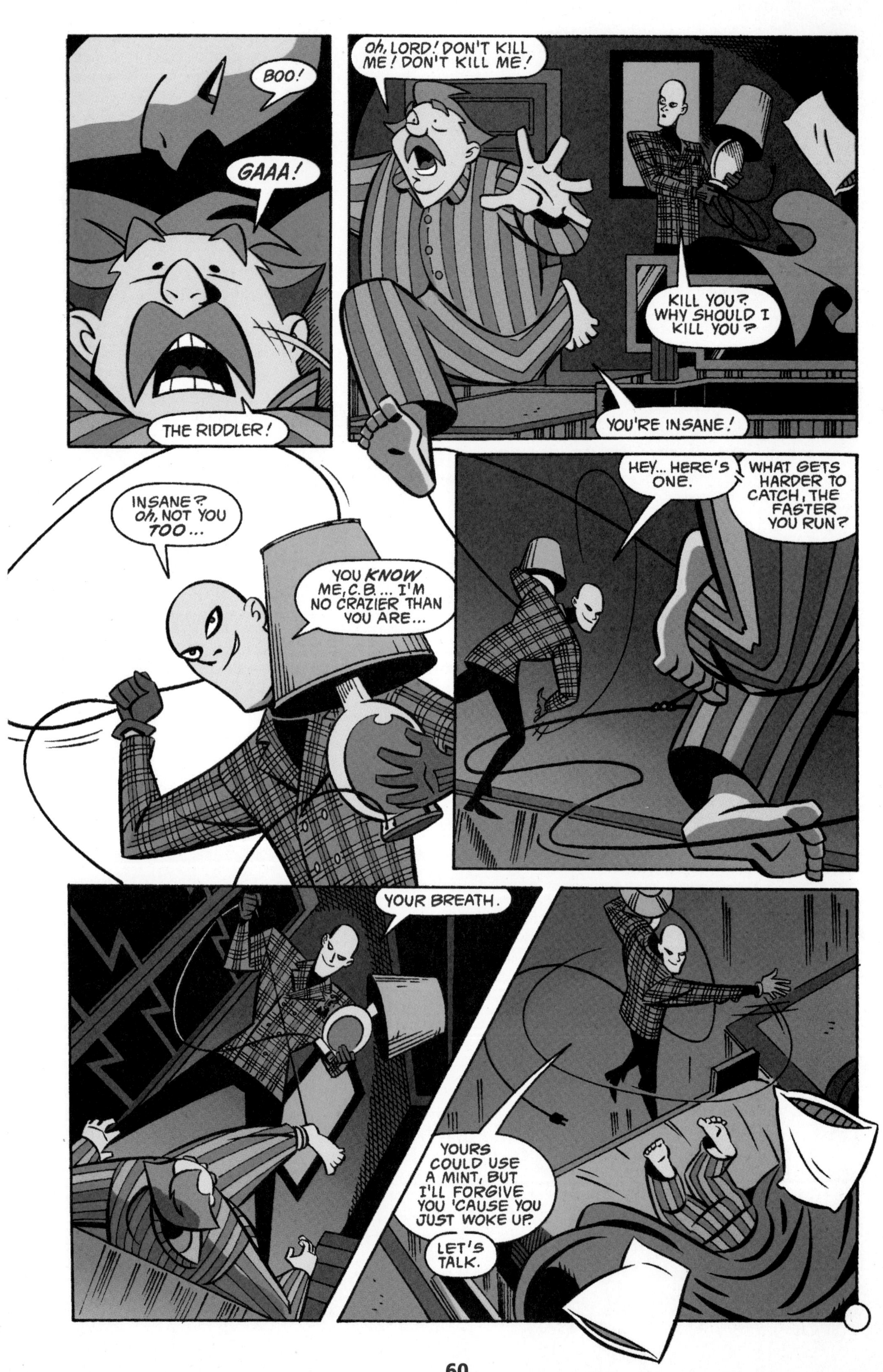
BOO!
GAAA!
THE RIDDLER!
Oh, LORD! DON'T KILL ME! DON'T KILL ME!
KILL YOU? WHY SHOULD I KILL YOU?
YOU'RE INSANE!
INSANE? Oh, NOT YOU TOO...
YOU KNOW ME, C.B. ... I'M NO CRAZIER THAN YOU ARE...
HEY... HERE'S ONE.
WHAT GETS HARDER TO CATCH, THE FASTER YOU RUN?
YOUR BREATH.
YOURS COULD USE A MINT, BUT I'LL FORGIVE YOU 'CAUSE YOU JUST WOKE UP.
LET'S TALK.

I JUST BROKE OUT OF ARKHAM AND I NEED A PLACE TO STAY... WELL, HIDE REALLY.
YOU'RE A RICH MAN WITH LOTS OF REAL ESTATE AND HOTELS... AND I WAS THINKING...
KLIK!
LOOK, NYGMA.

...I MAY HAVE HIRED YOU TO BE A SPOKESMAN FOR WACKO TOYS, BUT YOUR CRIMINAL BEHAVIOR BANKRUPTED THE COMPANY AND NEARLY RUINED ME PERSONALLY.
YOU HAVE NO FRIENDS HERE.

Oh, YOU WANT TO BE MY FRIEND, C.B.
SEE, I KNOW ALL YOUR SECRETS.

WHEN I WORKED FOR YOU, I USED TO HACK INTO YOUR CORPORATE FINANCE ACCOUNTS FOR SPENDING MONEY ALL THE TIME.
DON'T LOOK SO SHOCKED ...COMPUTERS AND PROBLEM SOLVING ARE WHAT I DO BEST.

BUT YOU WERE A BUSY LITTLE DEVIL, WEREN'T YA? SKIMMING BIG TIME FROM THE STOCKHOLDERS.
I BET IT WASN'T ME THAT BANKRUPTED THE COMPANY, hmm?
YOU CAN'T PROVE ANYTHING.

DON'T YOU BELIEVE IT, CHUCK. I KEEP RECORDS.
DON'T WORRY, THOUGH. YOU BUY MY SILENCE WITH A PLACE TO STAY.
SOMEWHERE STYLISH, LIKE THE PENTHOUSE OF YOUR NEW HOTEL.

THE CLEOPATRA?
YUP. READ ABOUT IT IN A MAGAZINE, AND I HAVE A THING FOR MYTHOLOGY.
I'LL STOCK THE FRIDGE... YOU KEEP THE STAFF OFF THE TOP FLOOR, AND YOUR SECRET'S SAFE. I'LL NEED CABLE AND INTERNET, TOO.

ALL RIGHT. I'LL INSTRUCT MY EMPLOYEES BECAUSE I KNOW THIS IS ONLY TEMPORARY.
YOUR COMPULSION TO LEAVE CLUES FOR BATMAN WILL SEE TO THAT.

WHATEVER CRIME SPREE YOU'RE PLANNING, HE'LL CATCH YOU AND SEND YOUR SICK CARCASS BACK TO ARKHAM QUICK ENOUGH.
GOOD RIDDANCE.

NO. I'M *NOT* GOING BACK TO THE *ASYLUM*. NOT THIS TIME... NOT EVER.
SEE, *THIS* TIME I'M NOT *PLANNING* ANY CRIMES...

...JUST CLUES.

"I FOUND THIS IN MY EMAIL BOX THIS MORNING."
LET ME PLAY IT FOR YOU...
NO, WAIT... THAT'S NOT IT.
TRY HITTING "ENTER."
KLICK KLICK KLICK
OKAY, THERE...
I THINK,
WAIT...
I HATE COMPUTERS.
HEY THERE, HO THERE, BATMAN...
I'VE GROWN TIRED OF THE GAME WHERE I DROP HINTS AND YOU APPREHEND ME.
SO. I'VE CHANGED THE RULES A LITTLE...
I'VE GIVEN UP CRIME TO START GIVING YOU A HAND AT YOUR DETECTIVE GAME.
MY RIDDLES WILL STILL LEAD TO CRIMINALS... THEY JUST WON'T BE ME. GET IT?
A Winter, a king, the pair are the thing,
To start up the sunrise crowd hopping.
The high and the low card runs all 'round the yard,
Without ever starting or stopping.
Try 5:30 am.
GET THIS ONE, AND YOU'LL RID GOTHAM OF A FEW BAD BOYS.
BUT YOU STILL WON'T HAVE A CLUE WHERE I AM... heh heh heh.
A Winter, a king, the pair are the thing,
To start up the sunrise crowd hopping.
The high and the low card runs all 'round the yard,
Without ever starting or stopping.
Try 5:30 am.

LIKE I BELIEVE THAT. NO MORE CRIMES FOR THE RIDDLER?
BATMAN...?

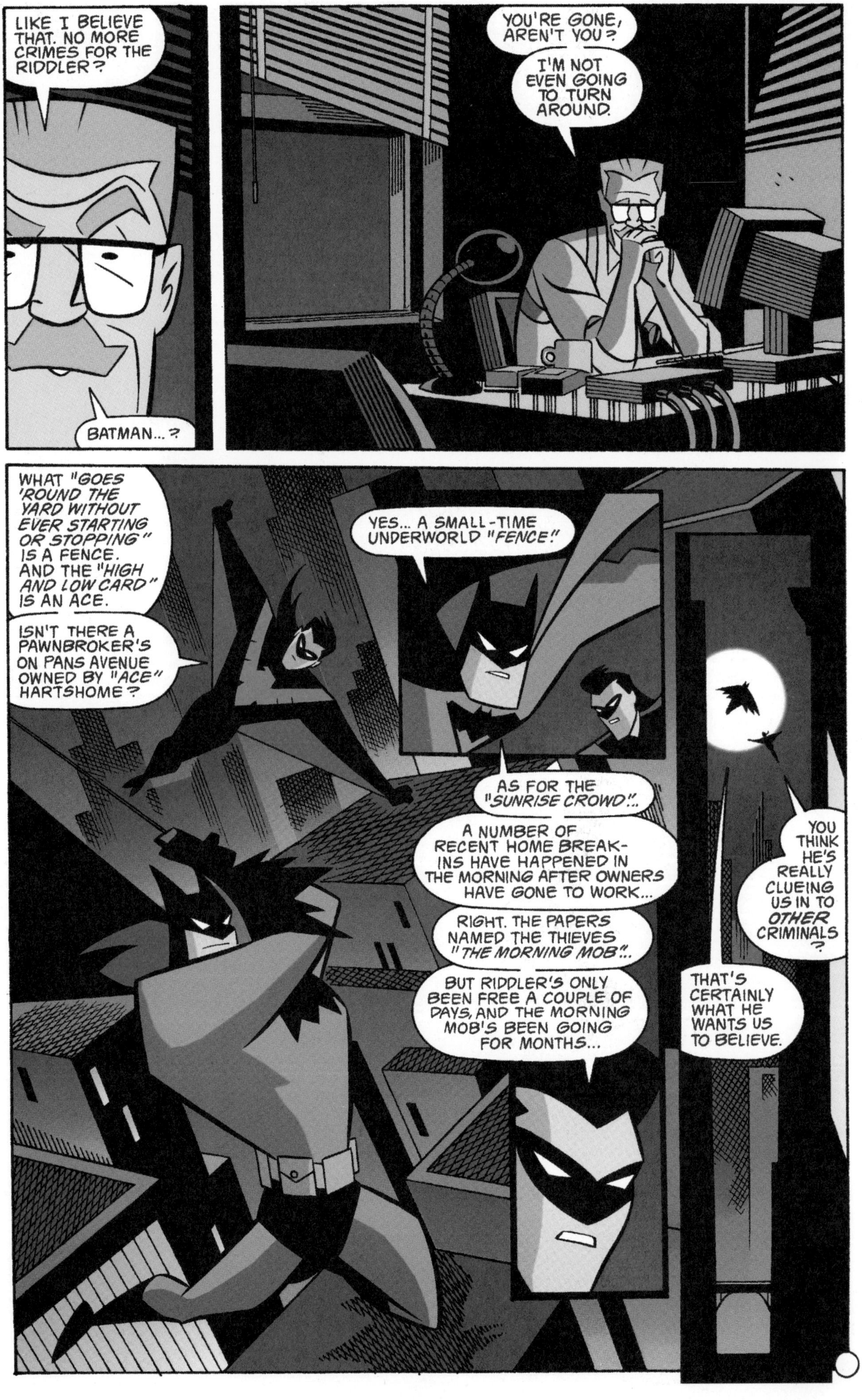

YOU'RE GONE, AREN'T YOU?
I'M NOT EVEN GOING TO TURN AROUND.

WHAT *"GOES 'ROUND THE YARD WITHOUT EVER STARTING OR STOPPING"* IS A FENCE. AND THE *"HIGH AND LOW CARD"* IS AN ACE.

ISN'T THERE A PAWNBROKER'S ON PANS AVENUE OWNED BY *"ACE"* HARTSHOME?

YES... A SMALL-TIME UNDERWORLD *"FENCE!"*

AS FOR THE *"SUNRISE CROWD"*...

A NUMBER OF RECENT HOME BREAK-INS HAVE HAPPENED IN THE MORNING AFTER OWNERS HAVE GONE TO WORK...

RIGHT. THE PAPERS NAMED THE THIEVES *"THE MORNING MOB"*...

BUT RIDDLER'S ONLY BEEN FREE A COUPLE OF DAYS, AND THE MORNING MOB'S BEEN GOING FOR MONTHS...

YOU THINK HE'S REALLY CLUEING US IN TO *OTHER* CRIMINALS?

THAT'S CERTAINLY WHAT HE WANTS US TO BELIEVE.

FIVE THIRTY. ZERO HOUR. QUIET AS A TOMB.
NO... DOWN THERE.

I BELIEVE THOSE TWO ARE ANDREW WINTERS AND MAX KING. A PAIR OF SECOND-STORY THIEVES.
AND THERE'S OUR "ACE" COMING OUT OF HIS HOLE.

THAT'S ALL THE PLAYERS IN OUR RIDDLE.
LET'S GO!

BATMAN?!?
SOMEONE MUST HAVE RATTED US OUT!

K-POW!

YOU LOOK LIKE THE BRAINS OF THE OUTFIT, MAXIE.
ANDY'S RIDING ON YOUR COATTAILS...
MIND IF I TRY?
SLAM!
WHAT HAVE WE HERE?
PAWNING THE FAMILY SILVER AT THIS HOUR?
IT MUST BE LOOT FROM LAST NIGHT.
ON THEIR WAY TO DO THIS MORNING'S JOB...
BUT NO SIGN OF THE RIDDLER.

WONDERFUL.
I NEVER REALIZED HOW MUCH I LOVED IT WHEN BATMAN SOLVED MY RIDDLES.

I WAS USUALLY TOO BUSY TRYING TO AVOID GETTING MY BACKSIDE KICKED TO ENJOY IT.

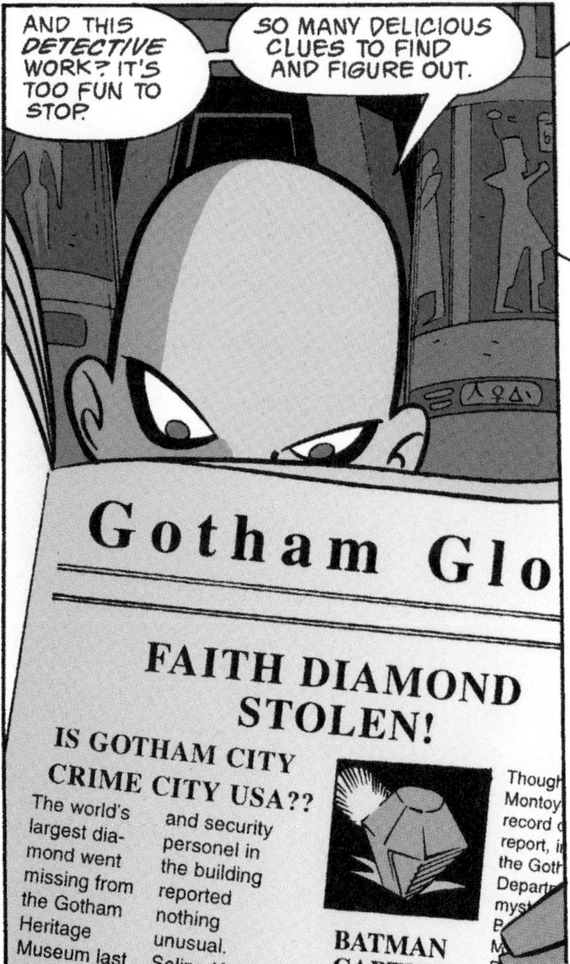
AND THIS DETECTIVE WORK? IT'S TOO FUN TO STOP.
SO MANY DELICIOUS CLUES TO FIND AND FIGURE OUT.
Gotham Glo
FAITH DIAMOND STOLEN!
IS GOTHAM CITY CRIME CITY USA??
The world's largest diamond went missing from the Gotham Heritage Museum last night. No alarms were tripped
and security personel in the building reported nothing unusual. Selina Kyle, the felon known as Catwoman
BATMAN CAPTURES MORNING MOB

THE MORNING MOB WAS ALMOST TOO EASY. I PAID OFF A COUPLE OF INFORMANTS AND I HAD EVERYTHING I NEEDED.

BUT NOW IT'S TIME TO DO SOME SERIOUS LEGWORK ON MY NEXT CRIMINAL INVESTIGATION.
SOMETHING MAJOR THIS TIME.

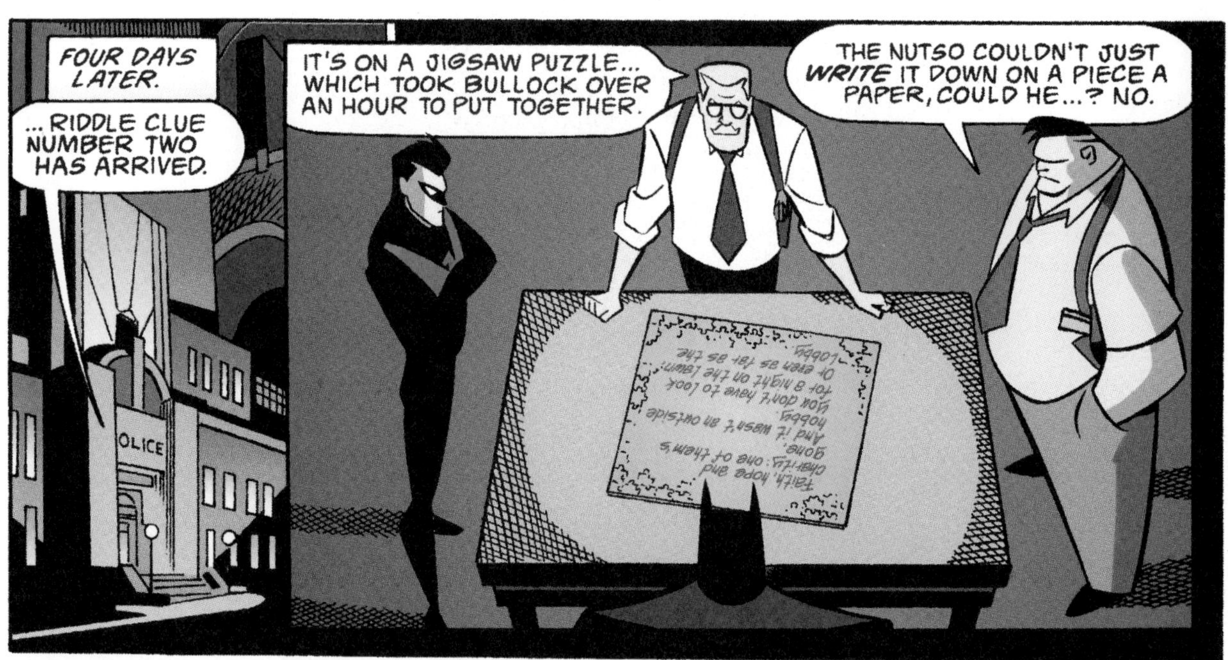
FOUR DAYS LATER.
... RIDDLE CLUE NUMBER TWO HAS ARRIVED.
IT'S ON A JIGSAW PUZZLE... WHICH TOOK BULLOCK OVER AN HOUR TO PUT TOGETHER.
THE NUTSO COULDN'T JUST *WRITE* IT DOWN ON A PIECE A PAPER, COULD HE...? NO.

IT REFERS TO THE MISSING FAITH DIAMOND.
Faith, hope and charity: one of them's gone.
And it wasn't an outside hobby.
You don't have to look for a night on the lawn,
Or even as far as the Lobby.

NOT "*AN OUTSIDE HOBBY*" MEANS AN *INSIDE JOB*.

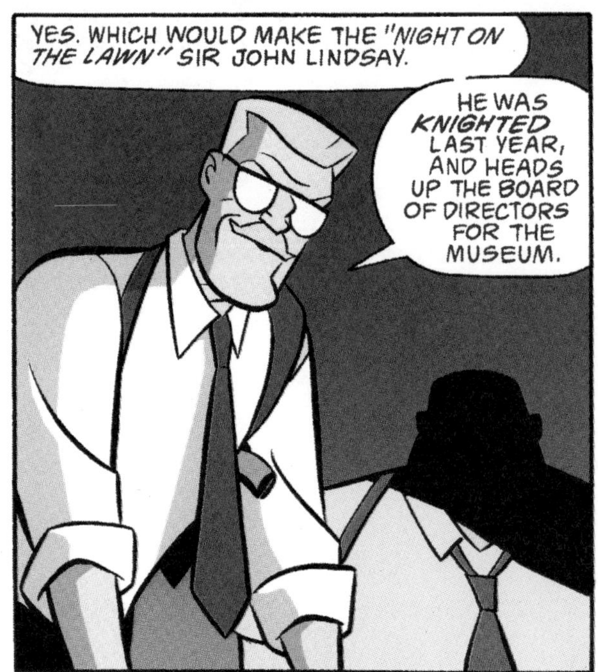
YES. WHICH WOULD MAKE THE "*NIGHT ON THE LAWN*" SIR JOHN LINDSAY.
HE WAS *KNIGHTED* LAST YEAR, AND HEADS UP THE BOARD OF DIRECTORS FOR THE MUSEUM.

WE DO SOLVE SOME ON OUR OWN, NIGHTWING. SIR JOHNNY'S GAMBLING DEBTS MADE HIM OUR #1 SUSPECT SINCE THE GEM WENT BYE-BYE.
BUT WE'VE HAD NO SOLID EVIDENCE.

THE REST OF THE RIDDLE SUGGESTS THE DIAMOND IS IN HIS OFFICE AT THE MUSEUM. THAT'S A LEAD WE DIDN'T HAVE.
I CAN'T GET A WARRANT BASED ON A CLUE FROM THE RIDDLER...

I'D CONSIDER IT A PERSONAL FAVOR IF YOU LOOKED INTO THIS, BATMAN. THE MAYOR IS ALL OVER ME ABOUT THIS ONE.

MUSEUM
EVENING, SIR JOHN.
EVENING, MALCOLM. I'M PICKING UP SOME PAPERS FROM MY OFFICE.
CERTAINLY, SIR.

"I THOUGHT GETTING INTO THE OFFICE WAS THE EASY PART..."

...BUT SIR JOHN'S SAFE TOOK YOU FORTY-FIVE SECONDS.
YOU SHOULD CONSIDER A CAREER CHANGE. YOU COULD END UP RICH.
NOT FUNNY, NIGHTWING.

NEITHER IS THIS...
JACK LINDSAY WAS A FRIEND OF BRUCE WAYNE'S.
WHO'S THERE?

WHAT ARE YOU DOING IN MY OFFICE?
WHY DON'T YOU TELL ME WHAT THIS WAS DOING HERE INSTEAD?

I WAS WAITING UNTIL A SECURE MOMENT TO REMOVE IT FROM THE BUILDING...

SCHWINGG!
I WAS HOPING TO DO SO NEXT WEEK...
BUT THIS CALLS FOR A CHANGE IN PLANS.

WHU--?

PERHAPS THIS CALLS FOR A LAWYER.

IT'S STARTING TO MAKE SENSE.

WHAT IS?

THE REAL CLUE.

RIDDLER'S UP TO SOMETHING BIGGER.

AND HE'S HIDING SOME KIND OF COMPLEX RIDDLE WITH THESE CRIMINALS HE'S SENDING US.

PAIR ACE KING JACK

FIRST, A *PAIR* OF THIEVES AND A MAN NAMED *"ACE"* AND *"KING."*

THEN A MAN NAMED *JACK* STEALS A LARGE *DIAMOND*...

RIDDLER SAID HE WAS GIVING US A *HAND* WITH OUR DETECTIVE *GAME*...

HOLY POKER FACES, BATMAN! YOU'RE RIGHT!

SO WHAT'S THE DEAL?
OUCH WITH THE PUNS. YOU'RE WORSE THAN HE IS.

I DON'T KNOW WHAT THE "DEAL" IS YET.
BUT AT LEAST NOW...
I KNOW THE RULES OF THE GAME.

A QUICK CRIME QUIZ FOR BOXY BENNET.
WHO WAS THE BIGGEST THIEF IN HISTORY?
ATLAS. HE HELD UP THE WORLD.
YOU'RE OUT OF YOUR TREE!
DON'T SAY THAT! I AM NOT CRAZY!
BUT I HEAR YOUR GOOD FRIEND "MAD JOEY" NOONE IS PRETTY NUTS... EVEN FOR A BAD GUY... NUMBER THREE ON THE TOP TEN MOST WANTED...
I'M NUMBER ONE OF COURSE.
MY SOURCES TELL ME HE'S IN TOWN.
AND THEY ALSO TELL ME YOU KNOW WHERE HE IS.
I CAN'T! I CAN'T!
HE'LL KILL ME IF I SQUEAL!
Oh... YOU ARE IN A TOUGH SPOT...
KKKZZZZZTTT!
BECAUSE I'LL DEFINITELY KILL YOU IF YOU DON'T.
AHHH!

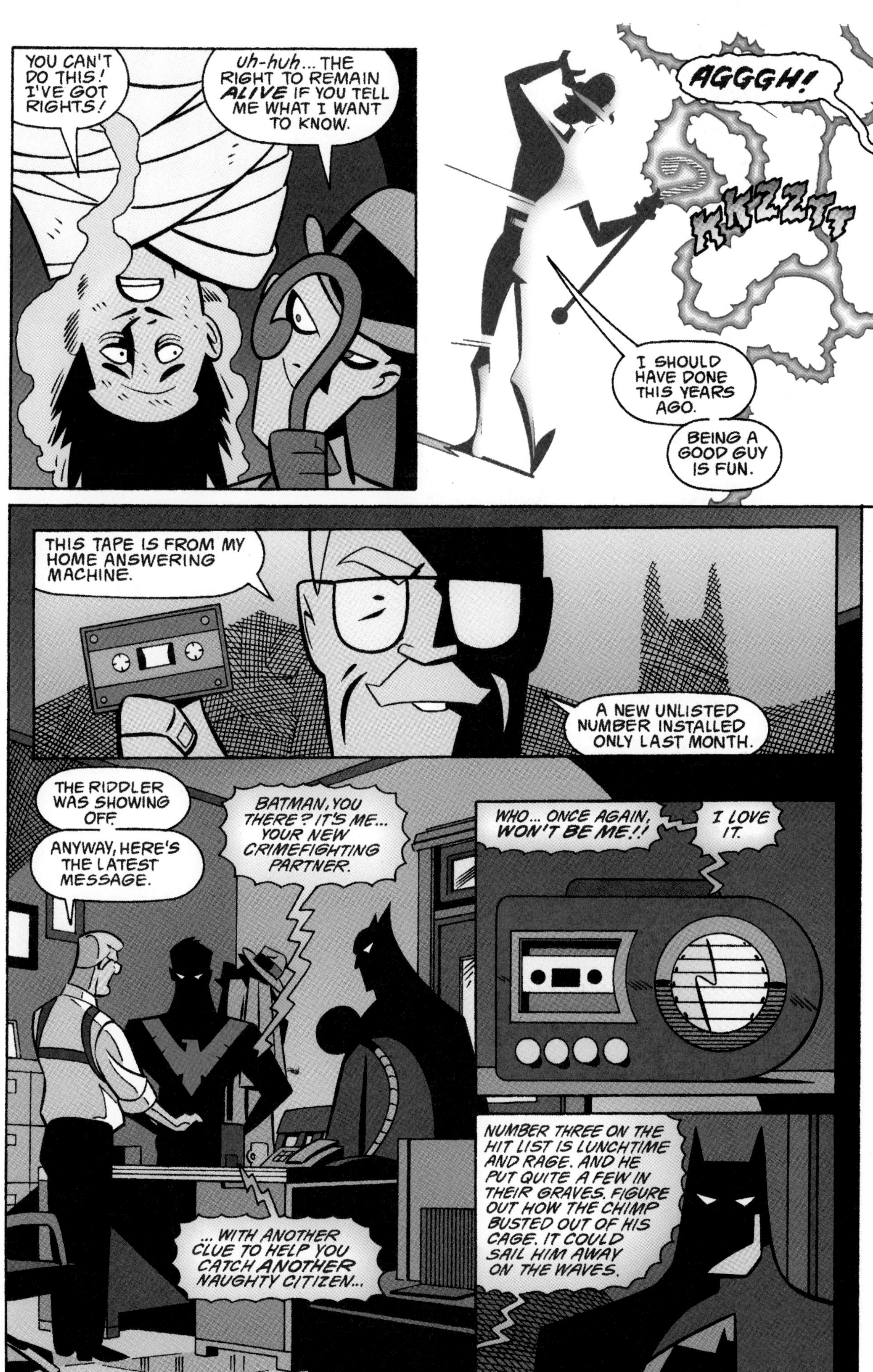
YOU CAN'T DO THIS! I'VE GOT RIGHTS!
uh-huh... THE RIGHT TO REMAIN ALIVE IF YOU TELL ME WHAT I WANT TO KNOW.
AGGGH!
KKZZZTT
I SHOULD HAVE DONE THIS YEARS AGO.
BEING A GOOD GUY IS FUN.
THIS TAPE IS FROM MY HOME ANSWERING MACHINE.
A NEW UNLISTED NUMBER INSTALLED ONLY LAST MONTH.
THE RIDDLER WAS SHOWING OFF.
ANYWAY, HERE'S THE LATEST MESSAGE.
BATMAN, YOU THERE? IT'S ME... YOUR NEW CRIMEFIGHTING PARTNER.
...WITH ANOTHER CLUE TO HELP YOU CATCH ANOTHER NAUGHTY CITIZEN...
WHO... ONCE AGAIN, WON'T BE ME!!
I LOVE IT.
NUMBER THREE ON THE HIT LIST IS LUNCHTIME AND RAGE. AND HE PUT QUITE A FEW IN THEIR GRAVES. FIGURE OUT HOW THE CHIMP BUSTED OUT OF HIS CAGE. IT COULD SAIL HIM AWAY ON THE WAVES.

THIS ONE HAS ME STUMPED.
THE CHIMP BUSTED OUT OF HIS CAGE WITH A "MONKEY WRENCH," RIGHT? IT'S AN OLD JOKE.

RAGE AND LUNCHTIME ADDS UP TO THE NAME, "MAD" JOEY NOONE.
HE'S A MOB HIT MAN WHO'S CURRENTLY NUMBER THREE ON THE FBI MOST WANTED LIST.

MAD JOEY'S A KNOWN ASSOCIATE OF BOXY BENNET'S...
... AND BOXY OWNS A YACHT CALLED, I BELIEVE... "THE MONKEY WRENCH."

IT SHOULDN'T BE HARD TO FIND OUT WHERE IT'S MOORED.
AMAZING.

WHAT IS?
HIS MIND. IT'S AMAZING.
Oh, THAT. YEAH.

SOCK! POW! WHAM!
MONKEY WRENCH

HEY, JOEY! HEADS UP!

KRACK!
UNGH!

THERE'S NO PLAYING CARD REFERENCE HERE, I DON'T GET IT.
CHEER UP. THIS IS A MAJOR LEAGUE FELON WE CAUGHT.
A LOT OF PEOPLE HAVE BEEN AFTER NOONE FOR YEARS.

AFTERNOON...? THAT'S IT!
I KNOW THE HIDDEN RIDDLE.
AND I THINK I KNOW WHERE TO LOOK FOR THE RIDDLER HIMSELF.

...I'VE JUST BEEN HANDED THIS BULLETIN...
WE HAVE A REPORT THAT MOMENTS AGO, FUGITIVE JOSEPH PATRICK NOONE WAS APPREHENDED IN GOTHAM CITY BY THE MASKED CRIMEFIGHTER BATMAN.

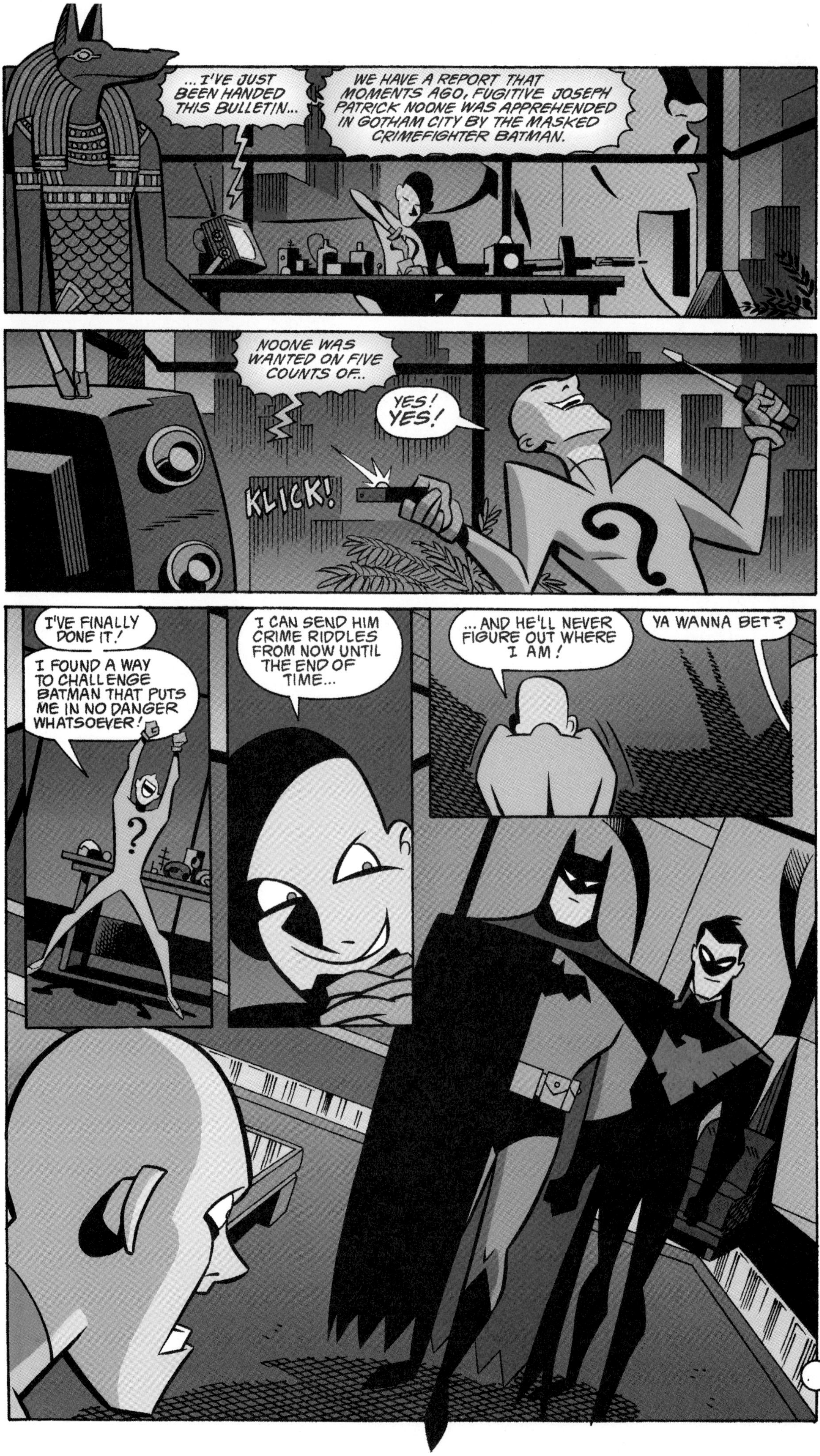

NOONE WAS WANTED ON FIVE COUNTS OF..
YES! YES!
KLICK!

I'VE FINALLY DONE IT!
I FOUND A WAY TO CHALLENGE BATMAN THAT PUTS ME IN NO DANGER WHATSOEVER!
I CAN SEND HIM CRIME RIDDLES FROM NOW UNTIL THE END OF TIME...
...AND HE'LL NEVER FIGURE OUT WHERE I AM!
YA WANNA BET?

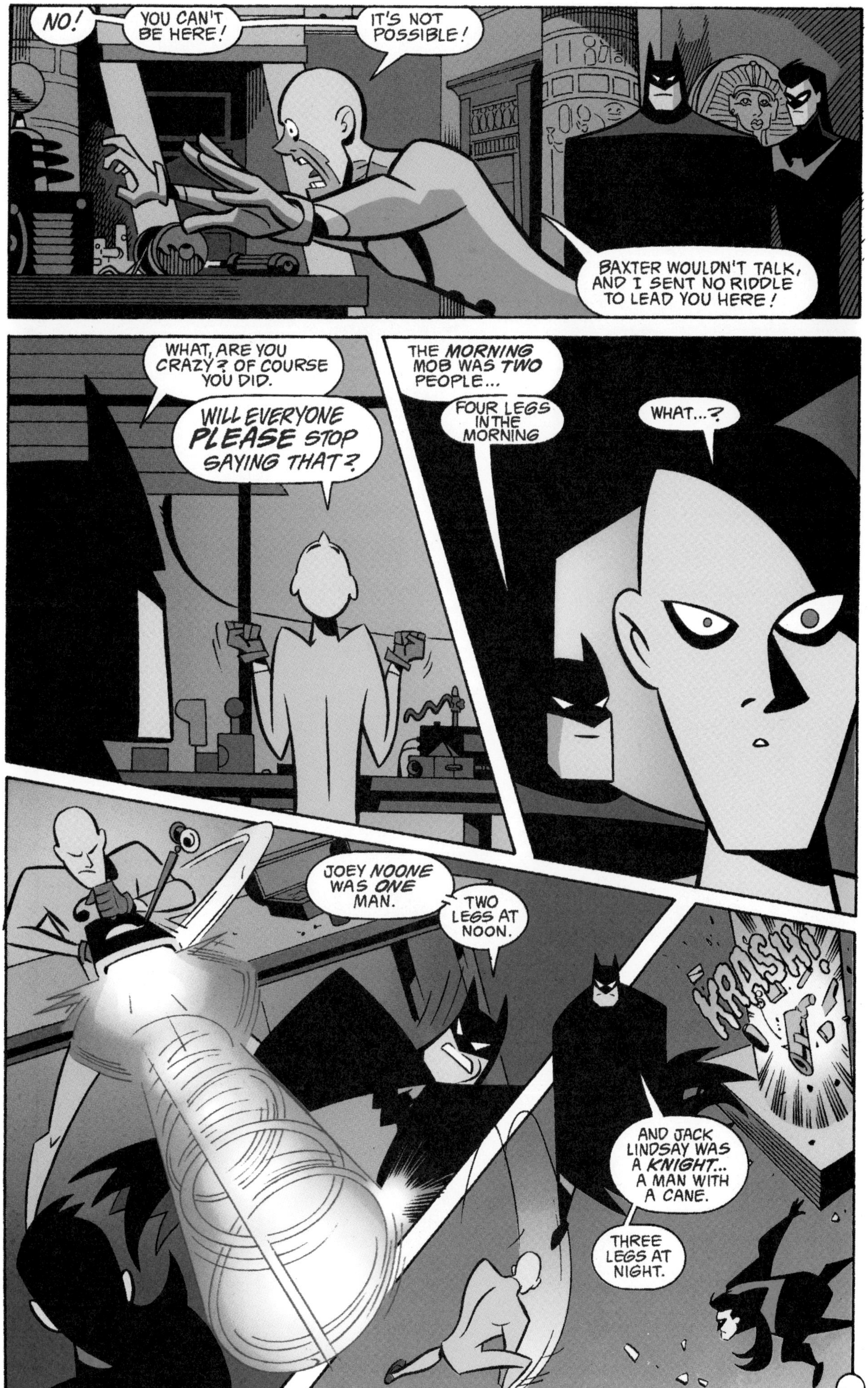

NO!
YOU CAN'T BE HERE!
IT'S NOT POSSIBLE!
BAXTER WOULDN'T TALK, AND I SENT NO RIDDLE TO LEAD YOU HERE!
WHAT, ARE YOU CRAZY? OF COURSE YOU DID.
WILL EVERYONE PLEASE STOP SAYING THAT?
THE MORNING MOB WAS TWO PEOPLE...
FOUR LEGS IN THE MORNING
WHAT...?
JOEY NOONE WAS ONE MAN.
TWO LEGS AT NOON.
KRASH!
AND JACK LINDSAY WAS A KNIGHT... A MAN WITH A CANE.
THREE LEGS AT NIGHT.

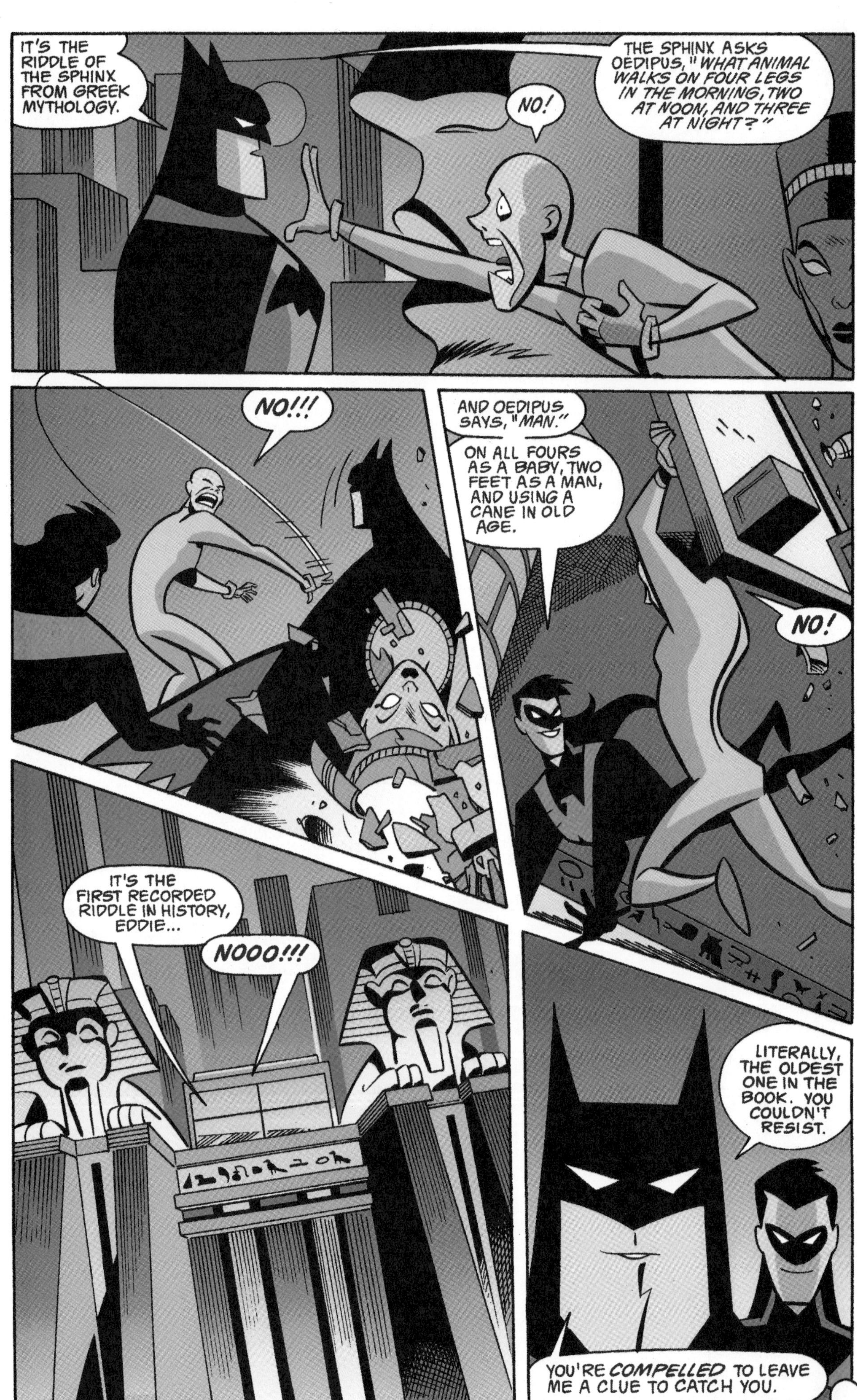
IT'S THE RIDDLE OF THE SPHINX FROM GREEK MYTHOLOGY.
THE SPHINX ASKS OEDIPUS, "WHAT ANIMAL WALKS ON FOUR LEGS IN THE MORNING, TWO AT NOON, AND THREE AT NIGHT?"
NO!
NO!!!
AND OEDIPUS SAYS, "MAN."
ON ALL FOURS AS A BABY, TWO FEET AS A MAN, AND USING A CANE IN OLD AGE.
NO!
IT'S THE FIRST RECORDED RIDDLE IN HISTORY, EDDIE...
NOOO!!!
LITERALLY, THE OLDEST ONE IN THE BOOK. YOU COULDN'T RESIST.
YOU'RE COMPELLED TO LEAVE ME A CLUE TO CATCH YOU.

AND THERE WEREN'T A LOT OF CHOICES FOR SPHINXES TO INVESTIGATE ONCE WE FIGURED OUT THE RIDDLE, RIDDLER.

WE CAME HERE FIRST, ACTUALLY...!
NO!

NO.

NO, YOU'RE RIGHT. I DID IT.

I DID IT-!

I DID IT!!
I DID IT!!
CRASH!
SMASH!

ARE YOU ALL RIGHT, NYGMA?
NO...I'M NOT.

YOU DON'T UNDERSTAND...
I REALLY DIDN'T WANT TO LEAVE YOU ANY CLUES.
I REALLY PLANNED NEVER TO GO BACK TO ARKHAM ASYLUM.

BUT I LEFT YOU A CLUE ANYWAY.
SO I...I HAVE TO GO BACK THERE.
BECAUSE I MIGHT NEED HELP.

I...
...I MIGHT ACTUALLY BE CRAZY...
THE END

"SUPERMAN'S POWER TRIP!"

PENCILLER: JOE STATON

"A WEEK IN THE LIFE OF LOIS LANE"

MONDAY:
SORRY, BOYS, BUT IT LOOKS LIKE MISS LANE IS GOING TO WRITE THAT INTERGANG EXPOSÉ, AFTER ALL.

TUESDAY:
SUPERMAN! THANK GOODNESS! ANOTHER FEW MINUTES AND WE'D HAVE SUFFOCATED IN HERE!

WEDNESDAY:
FORGET ABOUT ME, SUPERMAN! IF THIS BOMB GOES OFF, IT'LL TAKE HALF OF METROPOLIS WITH IT!

THURSDAY:
DON'T LOOK NOW, BUT I THINK THIS FLIGHT'S ABOUT TO MAKE AN UNSCHEDULED STOP AT STRYKER'S ISLAND!

FRIDAY:
WHERE...?
STOP LOOKIN' UP AT THE SKY AND JUST GIMME YER WALLET, LADY!
TUNE IN TO WGBS NEWS AT 11...

...FOR EXCITING FOOTAGE OF SUPERMAN'S SPACE-SHUTTLE RESCUE!
HEY, YOU HEAR ME? I SAID--
OH, FOR PETE'S SAKE...!

SOCK!
UNGH!

CAN'T COUNT ON ANYBODY SOMETIMES...!

PENCILLER: BRET BLEVINS

"ALL IN A DAY'S WORK"

PENCILLER: CAMERON STEWART.

"YET ANOTHER NINETY DAYS LATER"

PENCILLER: NEIL D. VOKES

(Almost) THE WORLD'S FINEST TEAM
BATMAN! YOU HAVE UNTIL MIDNIGHT TO SURRENDER YOUR COWL ON LIVE TELEVISION, OR BILLIONAIRE BRUCE WAYNE DROPS A COUPLE OF HAT SIZES!
WHAT IS IT TO BE, OLD BOY?
MARK MILLAR - WRITER
MIKE MANLEY - PENCILLER
TERRY AUSTIN - INKER
MARIE SEVERIN - COLORIST
ZYLONOL - SEPARATIONS
LOIS BUHALIS - LETTERER
FRANK BERRIOS - ASSISTANT EDITOR
MIKE McAVENNIE - EDITOR
SUPERMAN CREATED BY JERRY SIEGEL & JOE SHUSTER
BATMAN CREATED BY BOB KANE

THE MAD HATTER GOT BRUCE?
SLEEPING PILLS IN HIS TUNA CARPACCIO, AT THE GOTHAM ORPHANAGE BENEFIT LUNCHEON, MASTER NIGHTWING. WE NEED YOU BACK HOME IMMEDIATELY.
BUT I'VE ONLY JUST WRAPPED UP THE KILLER CROC JAILBREAK, ALFRED. EVEN IF I CHARTERED A PLANE RIGHT NOW, I WOULDN'T MAKE LOUISIANA TO GOTHAM BY TWELVE.
WHAT ABOUT ROBIN OR BATGIRL?
I'M AFRAID THAT'S OUR SECOND PROBLEM, YOUNG SIR. MASTER TIMOTHY IS IN UNIFORM, BUT I'VE LOST ALL COM-MUNICATION WITH HIM.
BATGIRL AND I ARE BECOMING VERY CONCERNED.
THE HATTER?
IF OUR LUCK SO FAR THIS EVENING IS ANYTHING TO JUDGE BY, I WOULD SAY THAT'S A RELATIVELY SAFE ASSUMPTION.

YOU KNOW, BATMAN, I'M THE FIRST TO ADMIT, THERE IS A CERTAIN SADISM IN MY ACTIONS HERE TONIGHT...
...AFTER ALL, THIS CEREMONIAL UNMASKING COULD HAVE BEEN A DIGNIFIED AFFAIR, FAR FROM THE PUBLIC GAZE. INSTEAD, I'VE OPTED TO PRODUCE THE TV RATINGS BONANZA OF THE CENTURY...
...WHERE I COMPLETE MY COLLECTION OF UNIQUE HEAD GARMENTS, AND GOTHAM CITY DISCOVERS YOUR SECRET IDENTITY.
Oh, AND DON'T EXPECT TO BE BAILED OUT BY ANY OF YOUR BAT-HELPERS, EITHER. LITTLE ROBIN TRIED AND FAILED, BUT THAT'S WHAT HAPPENS WHEN YOU SEND A BOY TO DO A BATMAN'S JOB.
TICK-TOCK, TICK-TOCK.
TIME IS RUNNING OUT FOR BRUCE WAYNE, CAPED CRUSADER.
IS YOUR SECRET IDENTITY REALLY MORE IMPORTANT THAN THE LIFE OF GOTHAM'S GREATEST HUMANITARIAN? SAY IT ISN'T SO!

NO SIGN OF HIM, COMMISH. MAYBE BATMAN'S WATCHIN' CABLE OR SOMETHIN' AND MISSED THE WHOLE SHOW.
OR MAYBE THAT SECRET IDENTITY OF HIS IS MORE IMPORTANT TO HIM THAN SOME WELL-HEELED PLAYBOY HE'S NEVER EVEN MET.
ABSOLUTELY NOT, SERGEANT BULLOCK. HIS METHODS MAY BE A LITTLE UNORTHODOX SOME-TIMES, BUT BATMAN VALUES NOTHING MORE THAN HUMAN LIFE.
MARK MY WORDS, HE'LL BE HERE.
I'M SURE HE'D APPRECIATE THE VOTE OF CONFIDENCE, COMMIS-SIONER.
BATMAN...?
BATMAN'S ON A CASE OUT OF TOWN, SIR, BUT I CAUGHT THE HATTER'S BROADCAST ON TV.
MIND IF I LEND A HAND?

GOOD LORD, NO. IT'S A PLEASURE TO FINALLY MEET YOU, SUPERMAN. I'VE BEEN FOLLOWING YOUR CAREER SINCE YOU FIRST APPEARED. BATMAN HOLDS YOU IN THE HIGHEST REGARD.
THE CLOCK'S TICKIN', COMMISH.
ACTUALLY, I WONDERED IF YOU KNEW WHY THE HATTER NEVER SAID WHERE HE WAS IF HE'S SO DESPERATE FOR BATMAN TO FIND HIM.
'CAUSE HE FIGURES ONLY BATS HAS WHAT IT TAKES TO HUNT HIM DOWN WITH ZERO CLUES. PRETTY SMART, huh?
YOU'RE DEALING WITH A DIFFERENT TYPE OF CRIMINAL NOW, SUPERMAN. GOTHAM CITY IS NO METROPOLIS.
PEOPLE HERE ARE TOO SCARED TO LOOK UP IN THE SKIES...
...AND BELIEVE ME, THEY HAVE...
Uh, COMMISH...? HE'S GONE.
Sigh
WHAT IS IT WITH THESE PEOPLE?

ANOTHER THOUSAND CRATES DELIVERED TODAY MUST BRING US CLOSE TO A MILLION BY NOW.
HE DOESN'T EVEN KNOW IF HE'S BEATEN BATMAN YET. HOW MANY MORE MIND-CONTROLLING HATS DOES THE BOSS ACTUALLY NEED?
I DUNNO. HOW MANY PEOPLE LIVE IN GOTHAM?
EIGHT MILLION, FOUR HUNDRED AND ELEVEN.
LAST TIME I READ THE PUBLIC CENSUS FIGURES, ANYWAY.
BATMAN! SPLIT AND RUN!
"BATMAN"? BOYS, I'M INSULTED!
I'M WAY CUTER!
KLONK!
OOF!

NOT FOR MUCH LONGER, TOOTS!
Ooh, NICE DIALOGUE...
THOK!
ANYONE ELSE FEEL LIKE TALKING? AS IN TELLING ME WHERE I CAN FIND THE MAD HATTER?
HOW ABOUT YOU?
G-GET AWAY! I DON'T KNOW NUTHIN'!
I WANT AN ADDRESS, CREEP.
YOU GOT ONE, BABY.
GOTHAM CEMETERY.

LOSE THE GUN, MISTER!
WHOOM!!
SUPERMAN-- AAAGHH!
OH, NO...
CONGRATULATIONS. YOU JUST SET US BACK A CRUCIAL TWENTY MINUTES.
EXCUSE ME?
WHAT BAT-CHICK MEANS, SUPERMAN, IS THAT THE VIOLENTLY PERSUASIVE TACTICS SHE AND HER FRIENDS EMPLOY AREN'T GOING TO WORK ON US SO LONG AS YOU'RE AROUND FOR PROTECTION.
WHAT MAKES YOU THINK I'M GOING TO PROTECT YOU?
YOU SEE MY FRIENDS BACK THERE...?

BLAM! BLAM! BLAM! BLAM! BLAM!
H-HEY. HE MISSED! EVERY ONE OF 'EM MISSED!?
I GET YOUR POINT.
DON'T TAKE IT PERSONALLY, SUPERMAN. I'M SURE YOU'RE VERY EFFECTIVE IN METROPOLIS, BUT GOTHAM HAS ITS OWN RULES.
NOW, IF YOU'LL EXCUSE US, I BELIEVE WE HAVE A SHORT STAY IN A COZY LITTLE CELL SCHEDULED WHILE YOU TWO KEEP LOOKING FOR OUR BOSS AND THAT KIDNAPPED BILLIONAIRE.
NICE TO MEET YOU, BIG GUY.

I'M GUESSING A MAN WITH X-RAY VISION IS UP TO SPEED ON *WHY* THIS BRUCE WAYNE SITUATION IS AN EXTRA-SPECIAL PROBLEM.
I REGARD PEEKING BEHIND MASKS AS AN INVASION OF *PRIVACY*, BUT BATMAN *FORCED* THE ISSUE WHEN I FIRST MET HIM.
JUST DON'T DO IT TO *ME*, BUSTER.
OKAY, OUR NEXT BEST HOPE OF FINDING THE HATTER JUST WALKED OUT OF THE *REFORMED CRIMINALS SOCIETY BAR*...
...JACK MOTEL, A.K.A. "THE REAL ESTATE AGENT OF EVIL." SEEMS THERE ISN'T A SOCIOPATH BREAKS OUT OF ARKHAM WITHOUT ARRANGING THEIR SECRET HIDEOUT THROUGH GOOD OLD JACK FIRST.
ZELLE CLUB
LEAVE THIS ONE TO ME.
OKAY, BUT REMEMBER-- YOU'RE IN *GOTHAM*.
THINK *"BATMAN."*
I CAN *DO* BATMAN.

GOOD EVENING, JACK. YOU'RE ON THE METROPOLIS TO GOTHAM FLIGHT PATH AT THE MOMENT, AND THERE'S A PLANE SCHEDULED TO CROSS THIS SPOT IN LESS THAN A MINUTE.
WHA-WHAT DO YOU WANT? WHAT DO YOU WANT?
JUST A LITTLE INFORMATION REGARDING THE WHEREABOUTS OF THE MAD HATTER.
TALK FAST, JACK. WE DON'T HAVE MUCH TIME.
I-I SWEAR, SUPERMAN! HE NEVER RENTED FROM ME! HE SAID HE WAS GONNA HOLE UP IN THE LAST PLACE ANYONE'D FIND HIM! HE SAID HE DIDN'T NEED ME!
HERE COMES THAT FLIGHT, JACK...
ON MY MOTHER'S GRAVE! HE NEVER RENTED FROM ME!

THAT FELT AWFUL.
WORD OF ADVICE, SUPERMAN. NEXT TIME YOU LEAN ON A SNITCH, DON'T BUY HIM A COFFEE AFTERWARDS. IT'S TOO WEIRD.
ZELLERS
EIGHT MINUTES LEFT AND NO SIGN OF THE HATTER OR ROBIN. THIS DOESN'T MAKE SENSE. WE MUST HAVE COVERED THE CITY FROM TOP TO BOTTOM A HUNDRED TIMES.
THE LAST PLACE YOU'D LOOK... THE LAST PLACE...
GOOD GRIEF!
MY THOUGHTS EXACTLY, BATGIRL...
"...THE ONE BUILDING WE WOULD NEVER THINK TO CHECK."
POLICE

CITIZENS OF GOTHAM--I REGRET TO REPORT THAT BATMAN HAS CHEATED AND ENLISTED THE HELP OF SOMEONE FROM WAY OUT OF TOWN.
THEREFORE, THE RULES OF THE GAME MUST BE CHANGED.
MY BACKUP PLAN IS NOW IN ACTION, WHERE ROBIN THE BOY WONDER, WEARING ONE OF MY MIND-CONTROLLING HATS, HAS BEEN COMMANDED TO CREATE A SUPERMAN-SCALE DIVERSION...
...INVOLVING THE BIGGEST PLANE HE CAN FIND, AND A TARGET YOU CALL THE HEART OF GOTHAM CITY.
CRASH HELMETS AT THE READY, BOYS AND GIRLS...
...I ESTIMATE YOU HAVE TWO MINUTES.
OH, YEAH...
LET'S PARTY.

ANY LAST WORDS?
HATTER, LISTEN TO ME! THERE'S SOMETHING YOU HAVE TO KNOW...
I'M SORRY, WAYNE, BUT NOTHING YOU CAN SAY OR DO ALTERS THE FACT THAT BATMAN HAS YOUR BLOOD ON HIS HANDS TONIGHT. AND ALL BECAUSE HE WOULDN'T PART WITH A BEAUTIFUL, STUPID COWL.
PUT THE GUN DOWN, HATTER.
I'M SERIOUS.
"BAT-*MAN!*" I SAID, "BAT-*MAN!*"
YOU CAN'T *POSSIBLY* BE SERIOUS, MY DEAR.
TELL THE BOYS TO BLOW HER *AWAY*, COMMISSIONER!

KEEPING ABREAST OF CURRENT EVENTS WITH YOUR SUPER-HEARING, MAN OF STEEL?
OR ARE YOU OTHERWISE DISTRACTED BY BOY WONDER'S KAMIKAZE MISSION OVER DOWNTOWN GOTHAM? POOR ROBIN CAN'T DISOBEY A SINGLE COMMAND SO LONG AS WE BOTH WEAR THESE HATS!
THAT'S WHY I'M SENDING HIM STRAIGHT TO HADES, AND HE'S TAKING HALF OF GOTHAM WITH HIM!

ROBIN! LISTEN TO ME! YOU HAVE TO CHANGE COURSE OR THOUSANDS OF INNOCENT PEOPLE WILL DIE!
THERE'S ONLY ONE GUY I LISTEN TO NOW, SUPERMAN...
...AND HE DOESN'T WEAR TIGHTS.
NO TIME TO BE GENTLE ABOUT THIS!
AUIGGH!

NOW PULL UP, BEFORE IT'S TOO LATE!
OKAY, OKAY!
ALL RIGHT, SUPERMAN!
YOU SHOWED THE MAD HATTER WHO ROCKS IN GOTHAM CITY!
WHOOP! WHOOP! WHOOP!
HEY, WHAT'S HAPPENING, S-MAN? LAST THING I REMEMBER WAS BEING CLOBBERED BY THE MAD HATTER. DOES BATMAN KNOW I'M FLYING HIS BAT-WING?
NO TIME FOR THE DETAILS, SON...

"...BATGIRL'S IN TROUBLE."
ALL I WANTED WAS TO STEAL HIS PRECIOUS COWL, AND HE'S TURNED ME INTO ONE OF THE BIGGEST MASS MURDERERS IN AMERICAN HISTORY.
OH, WOE IS ME...
WELL, WHAT ARE YOU WAITING FOR, GORDON? HANUKKAH?
GIVE YOUR MEN THE KILL ORDER!
I... I CAN'T...
OH, NEVER MIND!
OPEN FIRE ON THE CUTE CRUSADER ON THE COUNT OF THREE, BOYS AND GIRLS.
ONE...
TWO...
GO FOR THE HAT, BATGIRL...

WHACK!
ZZZT!
THREE!
DON'T WORRY ABOUT ME! JUST GET AFTER HIM!
HEY, WHAT THE HECK'S BEEN GOIN' ON HERE?
COMMISSIONER, ARE YOU OKAY?
I'M NOT GOING BACK TO ARKHAM!
THAT PLACE IS FULL OF LUNATICS!
OH, NO, YOU DON'T!
NOBODY GETS AWAY FROM ME THAT EASY!

OOPS.
PLOOSH!
MAYBE I SHOULD TAKE THAT BACK...
ANY LUCK?
ONLY THE BAD KIND, SUPERMAN.
THE ALLOYS USED IN SEWER PIPING ARE LEAD-BASED, WHICH NIXES YOUR X-RAY VISION...
...AND THE MILES OF TUNNEL DOWN HERE WOULD TAKE HOURS TO SEARCH EVEN WITH YOUR SUPER-SPEED.
GOOD THING I PAID A LITTLE VISIT TO THE BAT-CAVE BEFORE I GOT HERE, AND RAIDED THE WARDROBE.
HEY, CLEVER BOY...
"...ESPECIALLY WHEN OUR QUARRY IS KIND OF UNDER-DRESSED IN THE HEAD DEPARTMENT FOR THE FIRST TIME IN HIS LIFE."

BATMAN'S COWL, HATTER.
YOU WERE WILLING TO DO WHATEVER IT TOOK TO ADD THIS TO YOUR COLLECTION, AND HERE IT IS, BEING HANDED TO YOU ON A PLATE.
NO STRINGS ATTACHED.
I CAN'T IMAGINE WHAT YOU'RE GOING THROUGH OUT THERE.
THERE'S NOTHING MORE UNSIGHTLY THAN A HATLESS HEAD, AND THIS COWL IS SUCH A WONDERFUL PIECE OF ENGLISH CRAFTSMAN-SHIP...
YOU'D LOOK TERRIFIC IN IT. YOU REALLY WOULD.
OH, THANK YOU, SUPERMAN.
THANK YOU, THANK YOU, THANK YOU.
MAD AS A HATTER.
NO DOUBT ABOUT IT...
...BUT YOU DON'T HAVE TO BREAK SOMEONE'S RIBS TO SOLVE A CASE, BATGIRL.
INTERESTING IDEA.

THANKS. I ALWAYS APPRECIATE THE HAND.
"THANKS"? HE SAVED OUR LIVES, YOUR SECRET IDENTITY, THOU-SANDS OF CIVILIANS, AND BUSTED THE MAD HATTER FOR US, BOSS.
THEREFORE, I THANKED HIM. WHAT'S YOUR POINT, ROBIN?
PERSONALLY, I GET THE FEELING BATMAN DOESN'T APPROVE OF SUPERMAN'S FLAMBOYANT, WIDE-SCREEN TACTICS IN HIS HOMETOWN.
ON THE CONTRARY, BATGIRL...
"...SUPERMAN'S METHODS ARE VERY EFFECTIVE IN THEIR OWN WAY, AND THERE'S NO DENYING GOTHAM SEEMS A LITTLE BRIGHTER FOR HIS PRESENCE.
"I THINK IT DOES US ALL GOOD TO LOOK UP IN THE SKY...
"...EVERY ONCE IN A WHILE."
THE END

PENCILLER: CRAIG ROUSSEAU

"SUPERGIRL'S SECRET EMERGENCY WEAPON"

PENCILLER: BRET BLEVINS

"WHILE YOU WERE SLEEPING"

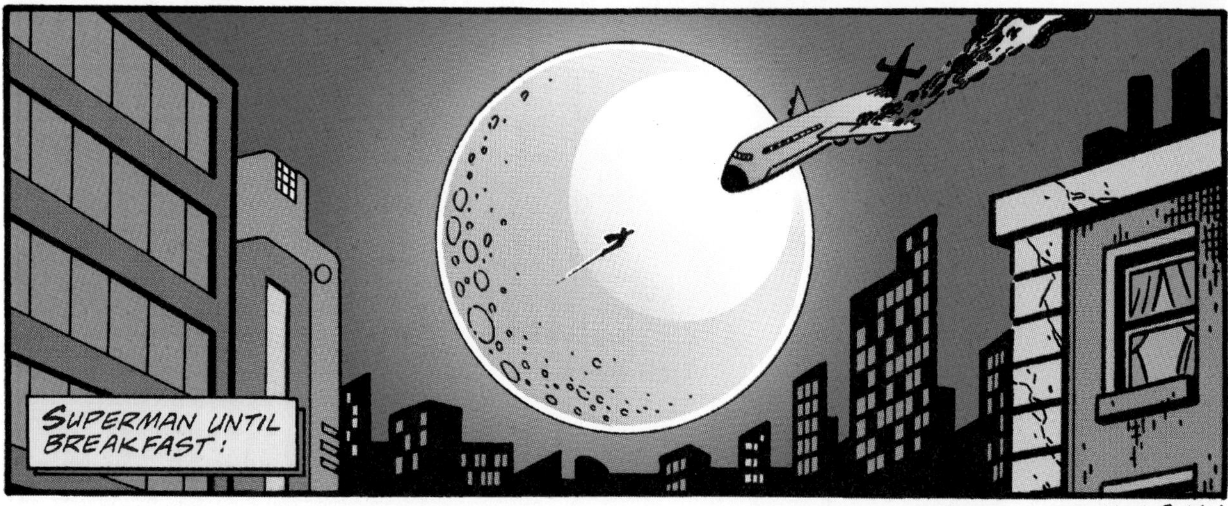

PENCILLER: MIN S. KU